CHARLES II

and

HIS ESCAPE INTO EXILE

CAPTURE *the* KING

CHARLES II
and
HIS ESCAPE
INTO EXILE

CAPTURE *the* KING

MARTYN R. BEARDSLEY

PEN & SWORD
HISTORY

AN IMPRINT OF PEN & SWORD BOOKS LTD
YORKSHIRE – PHILADELPHIA

First published in Great Britain in 2019 by
PEN AND SWORD HISTORY
an imprint of
Pen and Sword Books Ltd
Yorkshire – Philadelphia

ISBN 978 1 52672 572 1

Typeset in Times New Roman 11/13.5 by
Aura Technology and Software Services, India
Printed and bound in the UK by TJ International

Pen & Sword Books Ltd incorporates the imprints of Pen & Sword
Archaeology, Atlas, Aviation, Battleground, Discovery,
Family History, History, Maritime, Military, Naval, Politics, Railways,
Select, Social History, Transport, True Crime, Claymore Press,
Frontline Books, Leo Cooper, Praetorian Press, Remember When,
Seaforth Publishing and Wharncliffe.

For a complete list of Pen & Sword titles please contact
PEN & SWORD BOOKS LIMITED
47 Church Street, Barnsley, South Yorkshire, S70 2AS, England
E-mail: enquiries@pen-and-sword.co.uk
Website: www.pen-and-sword.co.uk

Or
PEN AND SWORD BOOKS
1950 Lawrence Rd, Havertown, PA 19083, USA
E-mail: Uspen-and-sword@casematepublishers.com
Website: www.penandswordbooks.com

Contents

Acknowledgements

I would like to thank two people who have walked in Charles' footsteps (or at least some of them) and kindly allowed me to use photographs they have taken along the way, and one group that provides the guidance to enable others to do the same. Gillian Bagwell has written a fictionalised account of Jane Lane's part in Charles' journey called *The King's Mistress* and has explored many of the places that feature in the story. Some of her photographs appear in this book, and many other fascinating ones can be found on her blog *Jane Lane & the Royal Miracle* www.theroyalmiracle.blogspot.com. Lucy Griffiths leads guided walks in the West Midlands and has trodden some of the same lanes as Charles and his companions in that part of the world. Again, she has kindly allowed me to use some of the pictures she took, more of which can be found on her blog: www.lucys-wednesday-walks.blogspot.com.

The map of Charles' route appears courtesy of the Monarch's Way Association. The Monarch's Way is long distance walk of 625 miles using footpaths and bridleways, closely following the route taken by Charles and taking in historic sites and buildings, two World Heritage Sites, one national park and six Areas of Outstanding Natural Beauty. The route is described in detail in three books by Trevor Antill, available only through the website www.monarchsway.50megs.com.

Finally, I would like to give a mention to my copy editor at Pen and Sword, Carol Trow, who is always a pleasure to work with and whose beady eye has helped to make both this book and my previous one (*The Gunpowder Plot Deceit*) into a much better finished article than I could have achieved alone.

Martyn Beardsley
Nottingham
February 2019

Introduction

The story begins in the George Inn, Mere, Wiltshire. Not King Charles' story, I hasten to add, but my own journey involving the researching and writing of this book. Although Mere is not my home town, it's a place I visit often and know well. I soon noticed that they make a big thing of Charles II in the George, including the displaying of a map of the route he took during his escape into exile after the Battle of Worcester in 1651, a 'King Charles' room, and, in one passageway, a rather surreal stone staircase fragment, embedded in a wall, commencing at about shoulder height, and rising for only about three or four steps before meeting more solid wall.

I later learned that although the George is a genuinely old building, this was just about the only remaining internal feature from the time of Charles' sojourn, hence the way it has been preserved and left exposed despite no longer serving any practical purpose. But I wasn't aware of any of this during my first forays to this quaint, friendly pub about twenty miles west of Stonehenge (another place Charles visited); I cynically assumed that all this 'King Charles' business was just a ploy to attract the travellers and tourists who tend to call at Mere to take a break from their journeys along the A303. But when I got round to investigating it, I discovered that not only was I wrong – Charles really did visit the George – but that the whole of his flight through England in search of a vessel to take him to France was more interesting, and at times dramatic and exciting, than I had imagined.

Some of the sources for what we know of Charles' odyssey contradict each other on certain points or dates, albeit mostly in relatively minor ways – it's acknowledged that even Charles' own account contains numerous errors – so I have done my best to recreate his passage through England by selecting and piecing together what seemed to me the most likely version in each such case. I haven't been afraid to incorporate stories from local tradition where they seemed to fit in with the known 'facts' as related by those who were directly or indirectly involved in the escape. I have only included dialogue which appears to be 'genuine' and handed down by

Charles or other contemporary, reliable sources – which brings me onto another point about historical veracity.

I want to stress that I'm very much against 'fictional non-fiction', that is, where authors basically make up stuff: what historical figures said or were thinking, what their facial expressions or body language looked like in a particular situation, and so on. This style, which sadly seems have become more common in recent years, is used by writers to give a factual account a more novelistic feel, presumably in the hope that it will have the effect of making their work will read more like a thriller and be more entertaining. Which it sometimes does – other than when, all too often, it reads like second-rate fiction! But either way, it is historically dishonest, even slightly desperate. More importantly, it means that there will be times when readers can't be sure whether Person A really did feel a tingle run down his spine or Villain B actually did glare at our hero with an evil glint in his eye and a snarl on his lips. Is it a matter of record, or has the author invented it to sex up the scene? You might say that it mostly doesn't really matter; but in my experience it creates a scenario where, sometimes even at important moments, we aren't sure whether or not literary licence is being employed – a far from ideal situation.

I relate all this at some length because I realise with sickening clarity that this book is the closest I have ever come to breaking my own rule. I took the risk mainly because I wanted to avoid simply rehashing previous accounts of this story, and also to some extent because I began to see that Charles' adventure genuinely does contain many of the kinds of ingredients seen in historical thrillers. *However*, I did draw myself a very clear line in the sand right at the outset, one I was determined not to cross. I don't know for a fact that the unnamed Royalist trooper 'spurred his horse on' in pursuit of Charles near Sidbury Gate, for example; neither is it written anywhere that Charles left the horse he was given at the door of his lodgings before dashing inside and out through the back in order to evade his pursuers. But rather than these details being plucked out of thin air, I thought acceptable to add them because of the balance of probability, and the fact that it would be a matter of great surprise if the rider *hadn't* spurred his horse on, and or that Charles rode through the house on horseback! These are the only kinds of liberties I have taken, and I faithfully promise readers that there are relatively few of them.

I've tried not to be too repetitive in my mentions of Charles' age and relative youth, but he is referred to as the 'young' king quite a bit. This was done consciously because I was aware that from my own perspective

INTRODUCTION

(I was so used to seeing the famous portraits of him in later life, a mature man in all his regal splendour) that as I was writing the book I had to keep reminding myself that my generally calm and stoical protagonist was a twenty-one-year-old with relatively little life experience. I don't class myself as a Royalist but couldn't help admiring the way Charles bore himself during the period covered by this book. I used the word 'adventure' earlier, but that is perhaps a little too flippant to convey the enormity of the situation he was in from start to finish. He was the subject of a genuine manhunt in unfamiliar territory, many miles from any sort of safety, reliant on outside help yet never being completely sure who could be trusted. What doesn't always come across in the historical accounts is that capture and almost certain death were an ever-present spectre hanging over the king and those aiding him at all times. An SOE agent trying to get out of occupied France during the Second World War might not be a bad analogy. So, and without any hint of hagiography, it's hard not to be impressed by the way in which Charles maintained not only his sense of humour but his composure and capacity for clear thinking; just about every decision he made turned out to be the right one – something which ultimately saved his life. This, then, is a tale of danger, hardship, close shaves and audacious bluffs – but above all of resourcefulness, loyalty and courage.

By the Parliament
A Proclamation for the discovery and apprehending of Charles Stuart, and other traitors, and his adherents and abettors

Whereas Charles Stuart, son of the late Tyrant, with Divers of the English and Scottish nation, have lately in traitorous and hostile Manner, with an Army, invaded this Nation, which, by the Blessing of God upon the Forces of this Commonwealth, have been defeated, and many of the Chief Actors therein slain and taken Prisoners; but the said Charles Stuart is escaped.

For the speedy apprehension of such a malicious and dangerous Traytor to the Peace of the Commonwealth, and Parliament doth straitly charge and command all Officers, as well Civil as Military, and all other the good people of this Nation, that they make diligent search and enquiry for the said Charles Stuart and his Abettors, and Adherents in this Invasion; and use their best Endeavours for the Discovery and Arresting the Bodies of them, and every of them; and being apprehended, to bring, and cause to be brought forthwith and without Delay, in safe Custody, before the Parliament, or Council of State, to be proceeded with and ordered, as Justice shall require...

London, Wednesday 10 1651

The Once and Future King

One early autumn day, Samuel Pepys received a summons from King Charles. Pepys was to join him at Newmarket, one of the sovereign's favourite places. This royal invitation was nothing unusual. Charles was an avid horse racing fan and a frequent visitor to that town, and most of his court often accompanied him. Pepys, in his role as Chief Secretary to the Admiralty, had worked with Charles and knew him quite well. In fact, he went to Newmarket with every intention of pressing his case for money that was owed to him. But Charles had other plans for Sam, and there would be no opportunity for him to pursue his financial claim.

On Sunday, 3 October 1680, Samuel Pepys and His Majesty King Charles II settled down together in the latter's rooms. With Pepys scribbling furiously using the shorthand he had employed in his diaries, Charles dictated the trials and tribulations of an extraordinary six week odyssey that had befallen him almost thirty years before.

Chapter 1

The Road to Worcester

Charles, Prince of Wales, was born into turbulent times. As Richard Ollard points out in *The Image of the King*, 'Few monarchs could rival his first-hand knowledge of low life… Before he was into his teens, he had seen the splendours of his father's vision rudely dispersed, his palaces abandoned, his capital closed to him, his Queen seeking asylum in France.'

Charles I had succeeded to the thrones of what were then still the three separate kingdoms of England, Ireland and Scotland and each brought with them their separate problems – mostly tied up in the struggles between the old religion, Catholicism, and the 'new' wave of Protestantism in all its different forms – a situation found not just in those countries but which was also mirrored elsewhere in Europe. This led to England's involvement in expensive and not always successful military operations, at a time of rising inflation. The way Charles I entered into these ventures and imposed taxes to pay for them with no regularly assembled Parliament to check him, caused increasing unrest.

Even though the complete breakdown of relationships between king and Parliament was still years away, at the time of Prince Charles' arrival in the world, his father was already embroiled in a series of ill-tempered battles with MPs and was becoming increasingly unpopular throughout the country. The year before Charles' birth, members had barred the doors to royal guards while it formulated resolutions against any change to the state religion and the raising of taxes without recourse to Parliament. Charles I's response was to dissolve Parliament itself.

Charles II was born on 29 May 1630, at St James's Palace. According to at least one source, thanks to the date being assessed for omens by royal astrologers, he was born at precisely 10.21 am. The same court prognosticators are alleged to have predicted bad things for the king in 1651! He bore the dark, even swarthy complexion that he was to carry through life. When he was christened at the Chapel Royal in Whitehall, all those present, by tradition, dressed in white satin trimmed with crimson. He and his siblings usually spent their winters at St James's, and their summers at greener, fresher and healthier Richmond. By the standards of the time, Charles' parents were loving and caring, and the affection seems to have been mutual.

Charles' mother was the Catholic Henrietta Maria, daughter of Henri IV of France. Despite the fact that the population of England still contained many pockets of staunchly Catholic (but largely patriotic) folk, this was still within living memory of the Armada and Gunpowder Plot and suspicions already abounded, especially among the increasingly influential Puritans, that the newborn prince's father might be leading the country back in the direction of Rome.

The young Charles survived jaundice, measles and scarlet fever to grow into a strapping young man, one able to look down on his rather short father – who liked to measure his children as they grew by carving a mark on a staff of oak (the first but of course not the last association between young Charles and that particular tree). So Prince Charles led a relatively happy, and obviously highly privileged, childhood; but the world around him was becoming increasingly turbulent.

Charles I continued to introduce unpopular taxes, and within a few years of being crowned King of Scotland he caused a major rift by imposing the Anglican Book of Common Prayer on a nation whose church was dominated by Presbyterians. In order to quell Scottish unrest, he was obliged to recall Parliament in order to raise funds to finance a military mission to the north. He did so, but it ended in failure. Parliament demanded that the king abandoned the unpopular tax he had levied on coastal towns to finance the navy; the king would only do so on the condition that he was promised the money he needed to pay for war with Scotland. There was an impasse, and Charles once again dissolved Parliament. A Catholic rebellion in Ireland only added to the king's woes.

The situation between Parliament and the king was beginning to look ominous, and Charles I began to prepare for the worst. Mindful of Henrietta Maria's religion and his son's vulnerability should a full-scale rebellion take place, he took decisive action. Henrietta was sent to the Hague (though she did briefly return two years later), both for her own safety and to raise Catholic support; and when the king abandoned London and headed north, he took young Charles, then aged around 12, with him.

Charles I formally declared war from a spot near the castle in Nottingham on 22 August 1642, setting in motion a conflict which would not be completely concluded for nine turbulent years. The ensuing English Civil War is divided into three phases: the first ending in 1646 and featuring a decisive defeat at the Battle of Naseby and the eventual imprisonment of Charles I; the second commenced in 1648 – Charles I was still a captive but had persuaded the Scots to invade, bolstering English and Welsh Royalist uprisings – and this phase ended with a Parliamentary victory over the Scots at the Battle of Preston in the same year, and the execution of the king the following year; the final phase ties in with the subject of this book: the Scots proclaiming Charles II as king in 1649, leading to their army invading England in 1651 with Charles at its head.

One of the notable features of this period was the emergence of the man who would become the nemesis of both Charles the father and Charles the son: Oliver Cromwell. Cromwell's rapid rise to military prominence and then political power in many ways parallels that of Bonaparte 150 years later. His transformation from eager officer to commander-in-chief was swift and well-earned. His eventual position of Lord Protector, coming after the death of Charles I and while Charles II was still in exile, is more controversial; but although Cromwell was one of first to sign Charles I's death warrant, he was not actually anti-monarchy. Quite late in the day he had been prepared to negotiate with Charles I, and even harboured a hope that he could be replaced by one of his sons.

To return to the early years of Charles II, despite his young age the prince was present at the Battle of Edgehill two months after his father declared war, where he came close to being taken by the enemy. There were some Royalist successes in the early stages of the war, but as the tide began to turn the king sent his son to the West Country, ostensibly as the military commander for that region, but with a council of experienced men to advise him. This wasn't an act of desperation. It wasn't at all unusual at that time for child royals to be given senior military roles and even take part in battles. Prince Charles' cousin Prince Rupert had started at the same age.

Royalist defeat at Naseby in 1645, in which Cromwell played a leading role, destroyed Charles I's hopes of ultimate victory, and in the south-west of England town after town fell to the Parliamentarians with Prince Charles and those around him heading further and further south and west to try to stay one step ahead of the enemy. When they could go no further on the mainland, young Charles was transferred to the Scilly Isles, but when a

Parliamentary fleet threatened that refuge too, he was on the move again. Even then, if it hadn't been for a timely storm which scattered the ships bearing down on the Scillies he might never have made it to his next haven, the Channel Island of Jersey, where he landed with a small retinue in April 1646. By then, Charles I had surrendered, and in late June, against the wishes of advisers but at the insistence of Henrietta Maria, the prince sailed for France where he was reunited with his mother and lived at the French court in Paris.

Despite being cousin to Louis XIV, who was only 6 and under the supervision of the Queen Regent Anne, when Charles arrived, he could not speak French. To be fair, his education had been somewhat disrupted by more pressing matters, to say the least. Henrietta Maria had a pet project of getting Charles married to his cousin Mademoiselle Montpensier, who was three years older than the prince. She also happened to be extremely independently wealthy. Despite Prince Charles' royal blood, it would have been a mismatch in just about every other way considering the depths to which fate had consigned him. He was a shy, awkward, penniless Protestant youth relying on the charity of a foreign court, who could not easily communicate with his 'intended' because of his lack of language skills; she was the wealthiest woman in Europe, who had the pick of the princes of that continent.

At around this time, someone in the French court gave a description of Charles: 'Well-made…his dark complexion suited his fine black eyes; his mouth was large and ugly, but he had a very fine figure'. Mmlle Montpensier herself said, 'He was very tall for his age, with a fine head, black hair, a brown complexion…'

Charles remained in the French court for around two years, becoming heavily influenced by the fashions and customs in a way that was to stay with him for the rest of his life.

Back in England, after a series of Royalist defeats Charles I had found himself besieged in Oxford. On 27 April 1646, in a move which foreshadowed the actions of his son he slipped away in disguise, initially intended to make for London, but finally turning north and surrendered himself to the Scottish army then at Newark. By the start of 1647 he had been handed over to Parliament, and after being moved between various locations during the course of the year, he staged an escape from Hampton Court in November. He took the risk of heading to Carisbrooke Castle on the Isle of Wight, in the belief that its governor, the Parliamentarian Colonel Robert Hammond, would help him flee to France. Hammond had become disaffected by the army's progressively hostile attitude towards the king and even Parliament itself; furthermore, Charles had once met Hammond, who had given him cause to believe that he was well disposed towards him. But it was a fatal misjudgement.

The king had put Hammond in an invidious position. With some reluctance, and after notifying London of Charles' arrival and being issued unambiguous orders by Parliament, Hammond placed Charles under arrest. Here, though, as in all of his places of arrest, Charles was allowed a fair amount of freedom – and he put this to good use by negotiating with the Scots and persuading them to invade England and put him back on the throne. But the Scots were defeated at the Battle of Preston in August 1648, Hammond was replaced, and Charles found himself in Windsor Castle facing a charge of high treason.

At the trial, in January 1649, Charles refused to plead. He was of the firm conviction that as king his authority came from God: 'I would know by what power I am called hither, by what lawful authority?' The court rejected the whole notion that he was immune from prosecution, and after hearing a succession of witnesses found him guilty and passed the death sentence.

On 29 January, the king was allowed an emotional final meeting with two of his children: Elizabeth, aged 13 (who died of pneumonia the following year) and Henry, 9. It being the middle of winter, before he was led St James's Palace to the scaffold outside the Banqueting House at Whitehall, he requested an extra shirt, fearing that if the cold made him shiver it might be interpreted by onlookers as quaking from fear. He made a final speech, then, removing his cloak, he turned his attention to the block upon which he would shortly lay his neck:

'You must set it fast,' he told the masked executioner (whose identity has never been ascertained with any certainty).

'It is fast, sir.'

'It might have been a little higher.'

'It can be no higher, sir.'

King Charles demonstrated to the executioner the signal to show that he was ready, which was to hold his arms out to the sides. He said a few words under his breath – almost certainly a prayer – then bent down and rested his neck on the block. When the executioner brushed some strands of Charles' hair under his cap, the king, believing he was about to swing the axe, warned him, 'Stay for the sign.'

'Yes I will, and it please your majesty.'

A moment later, Charles I reached his hands out. The axe came swiftly down, beheading the king in one go.

While the younger Charles had still been in exile, one sign that the tide in England was turning, and one which was to have an effect on his future actions, had been the mutiny of the English fleet anchored in the Downs in the middle of 1648. It came at a time of uprisings in England and Wales, which were ultimately to lead to a new outbreak of war. In the meantime, Kent was one of those areas affected, and here there were calls for the return of the king among naval officers and sailors. Royalist rebels took several towns, including Maidstone and Rochester, and the naval base at Chatham on the River Medway became a target. The unrest spread to vessels lying in the Downs anchorage, with ship after ship mutinying, forts overlooking the anchorage being taken, and Dover Castle finding itself besieged. General Fairfax's arrival managed to disperse the land-based rebels in Kent, but the nine ships which were in the Downs anchorage responded by setting a course to Holland in order to offer their services to Prince Charles and his younger brother James, who had ended up there after escaping England.

Charles himself now made all haste for Holland and assumed command, but internal rivalries among the senior people around Charles, and divisions within the crews themselves, meant that a planned invasion fizzled out ignominiously; Charles left them arguing with each other and went to the Hague. Scotland remained Charles' best hope of a return. With Charles I dead, the Scots had declared his son their king, Charles II. Discussions had taken place in 1648 for him to come, but the stumbling block then was the Scots' insistence on him taking the Presbyterian Covenant, which was at odds with his own Anglican views and practices. Presbyterianism is a form of church government which shuns the idea of the authority of bishops (Episcopacy, seen as 'popish'), favouring instead local assemblies of clergy and lay elders of equal rank. Charles's grandfather, James VI and I of England, had clashed with the Scots over this issue and gained some concessions. Charles I's efforts to build on that, which as we have seen included arbitrarily foisting the Book of Common Prayer on the Scots, went too far. In 1638, the Scots produced the National Covenant, declaring loyalty to the king but defending the purity of the Kirk, rejecting religious 'innovations' and anything it saw as having the flavour of, or a movement towards, Roman Catholicism. Charles I's response was to send an army northwards, the start of what became known as the Bishops' Wars of 1639-40. This resulted in an embarrassing failure, and Charles I suing for peace.

His successor now faced the same religious obstacles. Various schemes by Charles for a return were contemplated, started and abandoned, including a possible invasion via Ireland. Eventually, though, Charles swallowed his pride and to enlist Scottish help he agreed to accept the Presbyterian covenant in return for Scottish support. And it was a big concession, for the agreement he put his name to committed him to establishing Presbyterianism throughout England and the wording went so far as to harshly criticise the religious shortcomings of his parents. That he was prepared to humiliate himself in this way is a sign of the desperation and impatience he felt regarding the regaining of his English throne. He sailed for Scotland in June 1650, four years after departing Jersey.

Charles had a miserable time in Scotland, where he was harangued over the wickedness of his Catholic parents and forced listen to interminable Old Testament fire and brimstone sermons in the kirk – four times on Sundays. But it would be worth it if he could finally have his day, and after being crowned on New Year's Day, 1651 at the traditional site of Scone, preparations began for an invasion of England. By August, he had assembled an army and was almost ready to move – but it would not have been a sight to cause Cromwell to quake in his boots. It wasn't just that the force of around 8,000 foot soldiers and 2,000 mounted troopers would probably be numerically inferior to the army that Cromwell was likely to launch against him, nor his inadequate and not exactly state-of-the art artillery, (consisting largely of a few lightweight 'leather' cannon). It was the morale of his force. His senior military commander David Leslie, who had been against the invasion from the outset, was gloomy, telling Charles that he believed his Scottish force would not fight when it came to the crunch. He wasn't entirely incorrect. Many of the men they led were to fight bravely, but Leslie made his own prophecy come true by not engaging his cavalry during the battle to come, and eventually fleeing. After the Battle of Worcester, when Charles' escape was hindered and his presence in danger of being given away by the sheer number of cavalry around him, he would plaintively remark that 'I strove, as soon as ever it was dark, to get from them; and though I could not get them to stand by me against the enemy, I could not get rid of them now I had a mind to it.'

But that was in the future. For now, Charles and his largely Scottish army headed south having set out from Sterling, hoping to attract English support along the way. Reinforcements did come, though in far fewer numbers than hoped for, especially in the traditionally Royalist county of Lancashire. Charles' cause wasn't helped by the fact that a Scottish army had taken this same route three years earlier, plundering and alienating the locals as it went. Lord Derby did assemble a small Lancashire force, but on his way to meet up with the main army, it was intercepted at Wigan by a detachment of the New Model Army, defeated and put to flight. The New Model Army had come into being in early 1645 to replace the existing system of putting together a force made up of local militia. This was a system which would have been recognised by King Alfred: summoning a select number of men of varying degrees of training and equipment from any one region when the need arose. It could be particularly problematic when there was a need to move men away from their homes to fight in different parts of the country. Although the militia continued to play a vital role, the need for a professionally organized and trained national army was recognized and quickly put into effect. In the case of the Preston battle, the detachment was under the command of Colonel Lilburne. Robert Lilburne, a highly regarded officer from County Durham, had attended the trial of Charles I and been one of the fifty-nine men who had signed his death warrant.

Cromwell wasn't allowing Charles and Leslie free passage either, sending forces to harry them from front and rear and giving the order nationally to call out the militia to supplement the efforts of the New Model Army. By the time the invaders reached Worcester, English forces were swarming to Cromwell's aid from all directions, and the Scottish army was hemmed in by an army around double Charles' own in size. This was where he would have to make his stand.

Chapter 2

The Battle of Worcester

Charles had not planned on making a stand at Worcester. His first aim had been to reach London, where he expected to attract a great deal of support among Royalists and Presbyterians. But finding himself being harassed and monitored while still progressing through northern England, Charles' thoughts turned to the west, where he also harboured hopes of loyal backing. It was this change of plan and direction that brought his forces to the city of Worcester, where he intended a brief stay to refresh his soldiers and horses, and hopefully attract new recruits. But as units of Cromwell's army began to descend upon the area, it became increasingly clear that this was where the confrontation would take place.

While he awaited the inevitable battle against an ever-growing Parliamentary army, Charles worked to strengthen his position in Worcester by making impassable some bridges allowing access to the city across the Severn and the Teme and embarking on a massive effort to bolster the dilapidated existing fortifications around Worcester. Conditions in the overcrowded city were not good for the ordinary soldier. Worcester still hadn't recovered from being the last city to fall at the end of the first phase of the civil war; accommodation wasn't easy to come by, and conditions quickly became insanitary.

The Royalist headquarters were established in a medieval building appropriately known as the Commandery; the nave and cloisters of the cathedral were probably used to house soldiers, and the tower, with its excellent vantage point, made an ideal observation post for Charles and his senior officers.

Cromwell, in the meantime, was not only preparing for the coming onslaught but deploying elements of his forces to intercept any retreat or break-out from Worcester – particularly covering the route back to the north which the Scots might take should they break out, and the road south that Charles might use to advance on London. The net around Worcester was tightening.

Although Cromwell's forces were replenished by the arrival of militia and other English-based units, a large part of his army had had to make its way from where it had been previously engaged in Scotland, so was far from fresh. The first important engagement came on 28 August, when General John Lambert's cavalry rode south of the city to take Upton Bridge on the Severn, followed by the arrival of Major-General's Fleetwood's foot regiment to cover this objective and prevent it from being re-taken. The Royalists had partially demolished the bridge here but had left a solitary plank in place, presumably for their own use during the construction of an earthwork designed to defend the approach to the city. This seemingly minor oversight was to prove useful to the Parliamentarians, since Lambert's men were initially able to take the undefended bridge by stealth and begin repairs. Once the Royalists woke up to what was happening, an attack was launched, but despite a gallant and desperate attempt, in which General Massie was hit several times, it was too late and an important crossing of the river had been lost to the enemy. Lambert was able to send for a huge force from Cromwell's main camp at Evesham under Lieutenant-General Fleetwood to secure his gain.

Cromwell himself, with the bulk of his army, approached from the south-east and arrived the following day. He was able to occupy and command what had been the weakly protected high ground of Red Hill, from which his artillery could rain down cannonballs into the city below. That night, a Royalist attack on the artillery positions was attempted, led by Lieutenant-General John Middleton and Colonel Keith, but this foray was kept at bay. A further nail in the Royalist coffin was the assembling of bridges of boats which would allow Parliamentary troops to cross the Severn and Teme at a point close to a confluence between the two rivers.

The Royalists launched some sallies from the city, but these proved ineffective, and were in part sabotaged by Parliamentarian sympathisers among the Worcester populace, who were able to get news out to Cromwell's army both about planned sorties and the disposition of Royalist forces. One tailor who alerted the Parliamentary forces of one attack, causing its annihilation, was discovered and hanged in a prominent position to warn others of the consequences of betrayal.

Perhaps as a deliberate ploy to put the Royalists off their guard, the Parliamentary army did not launch an early attack on 3 September to follow up an artillery attack of the previous day as might be expected. But the units based away from the city were on the move, attacking Powick and its bridge. Bullet holes can still be seen in the walls of Powick church, the churchyard being occupied by Scottish defenders. The fighting was fierce; the first assault was held off and was threatening to stall, so using one of the bridges of boats to cross the Severn, Cromwell took reinforcements to bolster Fleetwood's men fighting in the fields and lanes around the village.

It was late afternoon by the time the Parliamentarians broke through and began to converge on the city itself. Charles ordered a counter-attack – partly encouraged by seeing that Cromwell had weakened his forces in the east somewhat to support Fleetwood. This move achieved some early successes, but it was not supported by Leslie's cavalry and was eventually repelled at great loss to the Royalists. For whatever reason, Leslie received no dispatches ordering him to act and seemed unable or unwilling to take the initiative. His force of around 3,000 horsemen remained loitering in a field to the north of the city. Neither he nor they ever took any part in any of the fighting. Historians have conjectured about the reason ever since, one suggestion being that Leslie had been defeated almost exactly a year earlier at Dunbar and didn't want to tangle with Cromwell again.

Charles left the safety of the city's fortifications, trying to protect his retreating men and rally his troops, but as the situation deteriorated and more and more enemy forces poured towards him, particularly those which had overcome the resistance at Powick and were now able to turn their attentions on the city itself, Charles was forced to take refuge within Worcester's walls. But the situation was rapidly spiralling out of control and soon there was little left for Charles to do but save himself. As he rushed towards his quarters he is reported to have said, 'I had rather you would shoot me, then keep me alive to see the sad consequences of this day.'

Chapter 3

The End of the Battle

After that the battle was so absolutely lost, as to be beyond hope of recovery, I began to think of the best way of saving myself...

King Charles, as dictated to Samuel Pepys

Late in the afternoon, with Charles' forces overrun and remnants fleeing in panic down the hill towards Sidbury Gate, one of Cromwell's pursuing cavalrymen who had become detached from his companions struck lucky. This archway was one of only two entrances into the walled city not now held by Cromwell's forces and it had become a bottleneck, as dozens and dozens of desperate men struggled to squeeze through the narrow aperture to the relative safety of the city streets within. Cromwell's lone trooper had spotted a tall, finely-armoured and dressed man vainly attempting to rally the Royalist forces and he realised that this had to be the day's star prize. Raising his sword and spurring his horse on, swerving around and over the hundreds of dead and wounded in that killing zone, he moved in to kill or capture the king himself.

*

A local worthy witnessed a worrying scene unfolding. 35-year-old William Bagnall was a clothier and city Corporation member – and, more importantly, a Royalist. He was lurking just inside Sidbury Gate, which was close to his house, holding tightly to the reins of his horse. He had taken refuge behind an ammunition wagon which had been overturned in the pandemonium, virtually blocking the entrance. Now, Bagnall looked on as Charles, fresh faced and fifteen years Bagnall's junior, recognising the imminent danger he was in, dismounted and scrambled beneath the vehicle and through the Sidbury Gate. As Charles was removing his armour, Bagnall quickly led his already saddled horse over to where the king was and proffered it to his desperate monarch. Riding along

Friar Street, Charles saw Royalist soldiers throwing their weapons away, and he went among them shouting encouragement. It was all in vain. Parliamentary soldiers were flooding into the city through other gates, and Bagnall watched as the king finally galloped away north through the city streets towards New Street and the house he had been using as lodgings near the Cornmarket.

*

Thomas Wentworth, the Earl of Cleveland, had also made it into the city. Cleveland was sixty years old, an experienced and courageous officer who had been imprisoned after the Second Battle of Newbury some seven years previously, when he had fought with Charles' father. He had commanded a cavalry regiment during the current battle. When he learned that the Sidbury Gate obstruction had been cleared and Cromwellian forces were now flooding through it (as well as from other directions) in pursuit of their valuable quarry, he knew he had to act quickly. He, Major William Careless, who had brought his own small force of horsemen to the battle, and other senior officers, gathered together as many men as they could and led a number of heroic charges down Sidbury Street and along High Street. Citizens of Worcester would later say that the streets ran with blood from the slaughter that ensued in what had now, these last-ditch charges apart, become a total rout. Cleveland was well aware that his small band was outnumbered and that what they were doing was an ultimately hopeless attempt at resistance – but that wasn't the point. The only intention was to buy time, to give Charles a chance to escape through Worcester's last exit not over-run by the Parliamentarians: St Martin's Gate.

*

Cromwell's lieutenant-general of cavalry, Charles Fleetwood, may not have known where Charles was or where he was heading, but he was acutely aware of the importance of St Martin's Gate. It was the only remaining way out of the city for the retreating Royalists, and he was determined to seal it off. Fleetwood was a Northamptonshire man in his early thirties, who had been wounded at Newbury and had fought at Naseby. He was to marry Cromwell's daughter Bridget is less than a year's time. After the fierce battle to cross the river Teme at Powick to the south, his men swept over the Worcester Bridge into the city and immediately made for St Martin's Gate. The net around Charles was tightening.

*

Three years previously, Lieutenant Colonel Ralph Cobbett had been dispatched to arrest Charles' father at Newport in the Isle of Wight and deliver him to Hurst Castle, whence he would eventually find himself back in London on trial for his life. Now serving as a major of the Regiment of Foot, Cobbett was chasing down Charles the son – and he was closing in on his quarry as he dashed through the chaotic streets of Worcester. Perhaps acting on intelligence, perhaps on prior knowledge, he and some of his men identified a large half-timbered house, with a row of gables facing the street, not far from St Martin's Gate. Cobbett and his party headed for this building, bursting in through the front door and commencing a search. The thunder of boots echoed on wooden floors as the soldiers scurried from room to room, desperate to intercept the enemy commander-in-chief before he could disappear into the Worcestershire countryside. With the ground floor checked and cleared, Cobbett sprinted up the stairs and came to a bedroom which looked out onto the Cornmarket. Here, almost as if it had been left to taunt him, he found the king's royal collar and garter, bearing the distinctive snake-like 'esses'. It is said that Charles had been slipping out of the back door as the major entered by the front. Cobbett would later present the royal paraphernalia to Parliament and be rewarded – but the biggest prize of all had escaped him.

Commentary

- More than 1,000 mostly Scottish soldiers are said to have lost their lives during the fighting around Sidbury Gate.
- Papers preserved by William Bagnall's family ruefully report that he was never recompensed for the horse or saddle. There are several other versions of the 'overturned cart' incident. Some say it was accidentally overturned, and even that Bagnall drove this vehicle (it's either an ox-drawn hay cart or an ammunition wagon, depending on the source) across the Sidbury gate himself. But if the situation had been as tight as described it seems unlikely that he would have had time to urge oxen to pull a heavily laden vehicle across the entrance, and then for him to overturn it, before the charging horseman arrived. It also seems unlikely to me that as a civilian observing the undoubted carnage that was taking place in that area, he would have been outside the city walls rather than inside. It is quite plausible, though, that the

cart, whatever its type, was deliberately overturned by Royalist defenders of Worcester in order to slow down the taking of the city. Bagnall died just a year later, at the age of thirty-six.

- Cleveland was taken prisoner again and remained in the Tower of London for five years.
- Cobbett, who almost caught Charles, was imprisoned by General Monck after the Restoration.
- Careless escaped, and he will reappear later in this story. He was a major at Worcester but in the accounts from which this story are drawn he is usually referred to by his ultimate rank (colonel). Thus, I shall be calling him 'Colonel Careless' from this point on.
- The house from which Charles darted out just ahead of his pursuers was owned by a Royalist-supporting family, the Berkelys. It still exists and at the time of writing is a pub called King Charles' House.

Chapter 4

Boscobel

The first thought that came into my head was, that, if I could possibly, I would get to London, as soon, if not sooner, than the news of our defeat could get thither: and it being near dark, I talked with some, especially with my Lord Rochester, who was then Wilmot, about their opinions, which would be the best way for me to escape, it being impossible, as I thought, to get back into Scotland. I found them mightily distracted, and their opinions different, of the possibility of getting to Scotland, but not one agreeing with mine, for going to London, saving my Lord Wilmot; and the truth is, I did not impart my design of going to London to any but my Lord Wilmot. But we had such a number of beaten men with us, of the horse, that I strove, as soon as ever it was dark, to get from them…

So we, that is, my Lord Duke of Buckingham, Lauderdale, Derby, Wilmot, Tom Blague, Duke Darcey, and several others of my servants, went along northward towards Scotland; and at last we got about sixty that were gentlemen and officers, and slipt away out of the high-road that goes to Lancastershire, and kept on the right-hand, letting all the beaten men go along the great road, and ourselves not knowing very well which way to go, for it was then too late for us to get to London, on horse-back, riding directly for it, nor could we do it, because there was yet many people of quality with us that I could not get rid of.

So we rode through a town short of Woolverhampton, betwixt that and Worcester, and went thro', there lying a troop of the enemies there that night. We rode very quietly through the town, they having nobody to watch, nor they suspecting us no more than we did them, which I learned afterwards from a country-fellow.

We went that night about twenty miles, to a place called White Ladys, hard by Tong-Castle, by the advice of Mr Giffard, where we stopt, and got some little refreshment of bread and cheese, such as we could get, it being just beginning to be day. This White Ladys was a private house that Mr Giffard, who was a Staffordshire man, had told me belonged to honest people that lived thereabouts.

King Charles, as dictated to Samuel Pepys

Waiting for Charles as he emerged from the house in Worcester was Lord Henry Wilmot, not yet forty but already a vastly experienced Royalist cavalry officer who had survived severe injury and imprisonment during the reign of Charles I. He had been ready with another new horse for his former sovereign's son, and with him were several senior officers, including the Duke of Buckingham, Lord Derby, and Lord Talbot, and nearby ready to escort them was a small force of about sixty mounted troopers. It was around six in the evening when Charles burst out of the house as yet unscathed. Wilmot's only concern from now on would be to save the neck of the man he hoped would survive long enough to reclaim his throne.

Once they had put about a mile behind them, they came to Barbourne Bridge, named from the brook which was a tributary of the Severn. Here they paused and took stock. Charles couldn't let go of the idea that the battle was not completely lost. Even with a force of just sixty, he pressed for a further stand. But Wilmot and the other senior officers felt they had to firmly disabuse him of this notion – especially as they could see that deserters were depleting his already small band, not to mention the fact that the Royalists had been greatly outnumbered even at the start of the battle. Wilmot also knew that Parliamentary soldiers were bound to be scouring the area in search of the king, and he hurriedly discussed their next move with Buckingham and his fellow commanders. And it was here that Charles was outvoted once more. He was in favour of turning south and making for London, but Wilmot and the others managed to persuade him to continue north, with the ultimate aim of reaching Scotland.

*

As the fugitives tarried nervously by the little bridge, their horses fidgeting and nibbling at the grass, the sun sinking over the western horizon, Richard

Walker found himself being summoned by his commanding officer, Lord Talbot. Walker was a trooper who had acted as scout-master (intelligence officer) to Colonel Sandys (who had been governor of Worcester when the city resisted a Parliamentarian siege in 1643). Talbot was aware that Walker had a good knowledge of the area they were heading into and asked him to act as guide. He readily assented, and at the head of the now rather depleted party and no doubt somewhat ill-at-ease to be shoulder-to-shoulder with his king and so many worthies, they set off. Walker led them in a direct line northwards, through the villages of Ombersley and on to Hartlebury where, tired and thirsty after the battle, they made a brief stop at a wayside inn, before moving on to Kidderminster. As they journeyed along the byways, they occasionally caught glimpses of the bedraggled remnants of what had been their army, streaming north on the main road.

*

As dusk turned to night on that September evening, Richard Baxter, a Presbyterian minister, had retired early for the night at his house in the market place of Kidderminster, some eleven miles from Worcester. He welcomed the gathering gloom because it gave him some relief from a troublesome soreness of his eyes, which made it difficult merely to look at anything in the full glare of daylight. But before he could drift off to sleep, he heard the sound of numerous galloping horses and guessed it was the remnants of Charles' army fleeing the battle he had heard about which had taken place over in Worcester. A detachment of Parliamentarians which had been guarding the medieval bridge over the Severn to the west of the town had arrived to intercept the fleeing soldiers; some submitted to arrest, others ploughed on and were fired upon by the Parliamentary soldiers. The firing of muskets kept Baxter awake till midnight.

*

The royal party were aware that the main route through Kidderminster was being used by members of Charles' routed army and that the place was bound to attract the attention of Cromwell's searchers, so avoided that town. Richard Walker continued to guide the retinue generally northward, crossing the River Stour in the vicinity of Wolverley, and about five miles further on to another stop at Whittington Manor. Another couple of miles, and they had crossed a heath and climbed the heights of Kinver Edge. This spot would have given them a good vantage point from which, as much as the fading light would allow, they might spot any pursuers. By now, though, it was between eight and eight-thirty in evening and darkness had set in. Walker had to admit that he had reached the limits of his local knowledge; someone else would have to suggest their next objective, and a new guide would be needed to take over from him.

*

James Stanley, the Earl of Derby, had arrived at the Battle of Worcester wounded and exhausted from the Battle of Wigan Lane just a few days previously. He had recuperated for a couple of days at a large, isolated house just inside the county of Shropshire. Not only was it owned by Catholics and Royalist sympathisers, but the family's delicate situation had led to them gathering about them a staff of loyal, discreet servants, and the creation over the years of various 'priest-holes' or hiding places for use in case of raids by the authorities in search of Catholic priests. In discussion with Charles, Buckingham and the other principal officers, Stanley suggested this dwelling, less than twenty miles to the north of their current position, as an ideal place to hide out for the night. But Stanley, who had been weary, bloodied and on the run when he had taken refuge there, didn't know the way back, especially in the dark. Another guide was needed from among their company to lead them to the haven of Boscobel.

*

Fortunately, Captain Charles Giffard, related to Boscobel's owner, was among those riding away from Worcester through the night with the king. Giffard was the owner of Chillington Hall, Staffordshire and didn't live at Boscobel himself, but another stroke of good fortune was that he had with him a servant who did know the paths they need to follow in order to get there. Giffard volunteered both of their services to the king.

*

Francis Yates was currently a trooper in Charles' army, but a 'husbandman', a small-scale farmer, who worked the land in the area near Boscobel in peacetime. He knew the general district well, and he had been sent to join Charles' group by Mary Graves, a local woman who had also supplied the king's party with several horses. Peering into the darkness, he led his illustrious companions down from the hill at Kinver in the direction of Stourbridge. Along the way, as the road took them down the hill towards that town, passing through the village of Wordsley, Yates and the others came across as an old gabled red-brick house, where the startled owner provided them with the only provisions he could – a drink and a crust of bread. It was a very brief halt and soon they were underway, but with Stourbridge just two miles off they needed to decide whether it would be safer to skirt it, as they had Kidderminster. Ultimately, they chose to press on through the town and elected to speak only in French if any conversation were necessary. But the decision nearly backfired when they discovered that there was a troop of the enemy stationed there. It was around midnight when Yates steered a very quiet and cautious group through the streets of the Stourbridge, and luckily the Parliamentary soldiers, no doubt exhausted from the day's battle, weren't on the alert.

After Stourbridge, Yates no doubt overheard the discussions between the king, Derby and Colonel Roscarrock (a Cornishman who had also taken refuge at Boscobel with Derby on his way to joining Charles), concerning going to that house and how safe such an isolated but known Catholic and Royalist place might be. As a result of this, the opinion of Yates' fellow guide Giffard was sought, and he suggested a house called White Ladies as a compromise. It was less well-known, and close enough (about half a mile) to Boscobel to allow communication between the two places. Yates and Giffard continued to guide the party in that direction. Having ridden at least fifty miles but probably substantially more, as the lightening eastern sky began to herald the breaking of a new day their path through the trees brought them in sight of what they hoped would be a place of temporary refuge and a chance to take stock and plan ahead; White Ladies. Francis Yates and Charles Giffard had now done their duty to the king.

Commentary

- The various old sources give several variations on 'Barbourne Bridge', which crosses a brook in the parish of Claines, including Barbon, Barebones, and Barbourn. The original bridge has since been replaced by a more modern structure.
- The inn that Charles and his adherents stopped at in Ombersley is still standing. It is now called the King's Arms, although early mentions of it call it the King's Head.
- It is often said that Walker got Charles' party lost, but I can't help thinking that this might be a little unfair. Thomas Blount, in his seminal work on the subject, *Boscobel*, uses the expression 'Walker was at a puzzle in the way', which isn't quite the same

as saying he had 'lost his way' in the accepted sense. A kinder interpretation would be that it was still dark, and he had reached the limits of the territory known to him.

- Charles later said that after leaving Stourbridge he rode with 'bread in one hand and meat in other'.
- Quite why it was felt that strangers travelling through an English town speaking French (as they did in Stourbridge) would be less likely to attract the attention of locals isn't clear.

Chapter 5

White Ladies

And just as we came thither, there came in a country-fellow, that told us, there were three thousand of our horse just hard by Tong-Castle, upon the heath, all in disorder, under David Leslie…upon which there were some of the people of quality that were with me, who were very earnest that I should go to him and endeavour to go into Scotland; which I thought was absolutely impossible, knowing very well that the country would all rise upon us, and that men who had deserted me when they were in good order, would never stand to me when they have been beaten.

This made me take the resolution of putting myself into a disguise, and endeavouring to get afoot to London, in a country-fellow's habit… There were six brothers of the Penderells, who all of them knew the secret; and (as I have since learned from one of them) the man in whose house I changed my cloaths, came to one of them about two days after, and asking him where I was, told him, that they might get £1,000 if they would tell, because there was that sum laid upon my head. But this Penderell was so honest, that, though he at that time knew where I was, he bad him have a care what he did; for, that I being gone out of all reach, if they should now discover I had ever been there, they would get nothing but hanging for their pains… The Penderells have since endeavoured to mitigate the business of their being tempted by their neighbour to discover me; but one of them did certainly declare it to me at that time…

So all the persons of quality and officers who were with me, (except my Lord Wilmot, with whom a place was agreed upon for our meeting at London, if we escaped, and who endeavoured to go on horse-back, in regard, as I think, of his being too big to go on foot,) were resolved to go and join with the three thousand disordered horse, thinking to get away with them to Scotland. But, as I did before believe, they were not marched six miles…but they were all routed by a single troop of horse; which shows that my opinion was not wrong in not sticking to men who had run away.

As soon as I was disguised I took with me a country-fellow, whose name was Richard Penderell, whom Mr Giffard had undertaken to answer for, to be an honest man. He was a Roman Catholic, and I chose to trust them, because I knew they had hiding holes for priests... I was no sooner gone (being the next morning after the battle, and then broad day) out of the house with this country-fellow, but being in a great wood I set myself at the edge of the wood, near the high-way that was there, the better to see who came after us…and I immediately saw a troop of horse coming by… In this wood I staid all day… and by great good fortune it rained all the time, which hindered them, as I believe, from coming into the wood to search for men that might be fled thither. And one thing is remarkable enough, that those with whom I have since spoken, of them that joined with the horse upon the heath, did say, that it rained little or nothing with them all the day, but only in the wood where I was, this contributing to my safety.

As I was in the wood I talked with the fellow about getting towards London, and asking him many questions, about what gentlemen he knew; I did not find he knew any man of quality in the way towards London. And the truth is, my mind changed as I lay in the wood, and I resolved of another way of making my escape; which was, to get over the Severn into Wales, and so to get either to Swansey, or some other of the seatowns that I knew had commerce with France, to the end I might get over that way, as being a way that I thought none would suspect my taking; besides that, I remembered several honest gentlemen that were of my acquaintance in Wales.

King Charles, as dictated to Samuel Pepys

George Penderel, the youngest of six brothers, heard an urgent knocking at the door of the gatehouse built into the walls surrounding White Ladies where he lived. Opening the door, he found himself face-to-face with his brother-in-law, Francis Yates, at the head of a small party of somewhat dishevelled yet very finely dressed men, asking to be admitted. George asked Yates if he had any news of the battle everyone had been talking about at Worcester and was promptly given the shock news that not only had the fight been lost and the king defeated – but Charles himself was one of this party, on the run from the Parliamentarians.

George quickly ushered the men over to the house of White Ladies itself, a substantial half-timbered mansion which backed on to the ruined Cistercian convent from which it derived its name. Even Charles' horse was removed from view and taken inside, where it was secured in the hall.

In the meantime, George Penderel sent a servant, Edward Martin, to summon his brothers William and Richard, local woodsmen. Upon their arrival, Will Penderel immediately recognised one of the men who had come to greet him, for it was the same Earl of Derby whom he had tended to when he had arrived in a wounded state on his way from the Battle of Wigan Road. Derby accompanied them to the main parlour and introduced Will and the others to their special visitor.

'Have as much care of him as thou hadst of me,' he urged them.

Worryingly, the new arrivals brought news of a band of local militia under Colonel Ashenhurst lurking at Codsal, around three miles away. The Penderels saw to it that Charles and his retinue were provided with a hasty breakfast of bread and cheese. During this time, George had to respond to yet another knock at the door. It must have caused some alarm among the inhabitants, but it was a neighbour come to report that there was a large body of Royalists nearby 'all in disorder'; some of Charles' officers tried to persuade him to join them and lead them as a force to Scotland, but Charles was sure the plan could never work and wouldn't entertain the idea. Having seen the way his Scottish cavalry failed to support him during the battle itself, he saw little prospect in them maintaining the discipline to undertake a fighting retreat so far north with an already victorious and motivated Parliamentary army snapping at their heels. Consequently, the decision was taken that Charles would fare best travelling as part of a very small group. The majority of the officers and the men under him would attempt to meet up with the remnants of the Royalists and head north.

The Penderel brothers then looked on as the young king bade an emotional farewell to the companions who had stood beside him in battle and helped to preserve him thus far, both sides probably knowing there was a good chance that they might never see each other again. In fact, the departing officers insisted that Charles not tell them his intended route or destination, lest they be caught and tortured into telling what they knew. They left to join the cavalry force – around 3,000 horse, they had been told of, which was currently on a heath in the vicinity of nearby Tong Castle. The only exception was Lord Wilmot, who, like Charles, planned to get to London.

The only hope for Charles was to travel virtually alone, and incognito. To this end, he would need a disguise. The Penderels happily rustled up some countryman's clothing for him while he stripped off his buff coat, (a thin leather jacket worn mostly by cavalry officers which provided some protection against the sword), linen doublet and grey breeches, as well as divesting himself of his blue ribband, his George of Diamonds (an ornament bearing the cross of St George picked out in diamonds) and all other finery that would betray his true royal identity should he be challenged or caught. Before long, he was kitted out in a coarse shirt (known as a noggen) offered up by the servant Edward Martin, who was a tenant at White Ladies. Will Penderel, being tall like Charles himself, provided most of the other gear: a leather doublet, grey cloth breeches, and a green jerkin. For his feet, a pair of shoes was produced by a man called Creswell, but these had to have cuts made in the leather to help them fit better – not a good sign in view of the arduous journeying that was bound to be in store for him. To top it off, the Penderels provided the king with a white hat with a 'steeple crown'. Charles also added some grime to his appearance by rubbing his hands against the inside the chimney and then smearing his face with the soot. To complete the look, Richard needed to rid Charles of his readily identifiable flowing dark locks, attacking the royal head with a pair of shears. The result was hardly stylish, but it wasn't meant to be and in fact Charles expressed his delight at Richard's hairdressing skills. He explained that this was because an earlier attempt at barbering by Lord Wilmot had been with a knife, and he inflicted upon Charles' scalp the only wound he received as a result of the Battle of Worcester.

*

Wilmot and Charles had privately arranged to meet again at the Three Cranes in the Vintry, should they both be lucky enough to reach the capital. That was neither here nor there to John Penderel, who set off with the earl to find a safe haven while brother Richard tended to the king. It was early days in the great escape; despite his overall goal, Wilmot had no immediate plan as to where to go, and this first stage of the search proved fraught with danger. As the two men passed the forge at Brewood, north of Wolverhampton, their appearance had an effect akin to disturbing a wasps' nest when iron workers, deciding that they looked like suspicious characters, came chasing after them. Luckily, they accepted the explanation that Wilmot was actually Colonel Thomas Crompton of the Parliamentary army. They had barely got any further along the road when, at Coven Brook, Wilmot and John Penderel just managed to avoid a group of Parliamentary soldiers. Even then, soon after they moved on, they realised that a group of horsemen was approaching them from the rear. The riders turned out not to be a threat, but all the same, the pair were somewhat spooked and, thanks to a chance meeting with a friend of John Penderel's called William Walker, they were taken to the cottage of a man called Huntbach at Brinsford. Upon arrival, Wilmot told John he still wasn't happy that this little dwelling was a good or safe place to hide out, especially if his stay might need to extend to a few days, so he sent John to seek an alternative.

He first travelled to Wolverhampton but being one of the larger towns in the area this was perhaps overly optimistic, and John found the place to be awash with soldiers – but the quest wasn't in vain because two subsequent chance encounters were to prove beneficial to the cause. John Penderel roved a few miles further north, and at Northycote he encountered Goodwife Underhill, an acquaintance. It was while he was chatting to her that Father John Huddleston, a Benedictine monk whom John knew and trusted from visits he had made to White Ladies. He asked Huddleston whether he had any news, and the latter replied that he had very good news – he had heard that the king had won the day at Worcester.

"Tis clean contrary,' John Penderel said. He took Huddleston, a Lancastrian in his early forties with long dark hair and matching bushy eyebrows, into his confidence regarding the arrival of Charles and also explained his immediate predicament concerning 'a person of quality' connected with the recent events. Huddleston was prepared to do what he could, and hurried to Moseley and one Thomas Whitgreave, a Catholic at whose house he acted as chaplain to his nephew and two other boys. Whitgreave had no hesitation in agreeing to give save haven to this important refugee; he quickly went over to Huntbach's house to offer his services to the man currently only John Penderel knew to be Lord Wilmot. Whitgreave believed they needed to take precautions, however, because of the Parliamentarian activity in the area and the prying eyes of locals. He arranged for Huntbach to lead his lordship through the back lanes to a field on his property, and Whitgreave would be waiting for him there at midnight.

*

Thomas Whitgreave, whose family owned White Ladies, was formerly a lawyer and had served in the rank of lieutenant under Captain Giffard (whose troop in turn was commanded by Lord Wilmot) during the civil war. He had been wounded at Naseby in 1645. He was now living with his widowed mother Alice, where he was already harbouring Father Thomas Huddleston. He waited patiently in his field in the dead of night, hoping and expecting to see the shadowy outlines of Huntbach and Wilmot emerge out of the darkness at any moment. But midnight passed, then one o'clock, then two. He returned home with a heavy heart – only to find that his anonymous visitor was already there. Upon quizzing Huntbach, it emerged that Wilmot's guide, either not understanding or ignoring the instruction he had been given, had taken his lordship by the main roads, and the latter was none too pleased. But they had got away with it and Whitgreave was able to show Wilmot into Moseley Hall. His was a Catholic family, and in the days when priests were ruthlessly hunted down, his forebears had taken the kind of precautions common in the homes of many better-off Catholics – they had had a priest-hole constructed in case of emergency.

Satisfied with this, Wilmot was left to rest for what was left of the night, while John Penderel was dispatched to Boscobel to inform Charles of Wilmot's whereabouts. Whitgreave's concern when it began to get light the next day was Wilmot's horses, since his house was situated on a main road and overlooked by that of his neighbour. Wilmot could be hidden away in the house well enough, but the sudden appearance of two fine horses might be noticed – for which reason they had been taken to the property of a neighbour of Huntbach's for the night. Whitgreave decided to send a messenger to his friend Colonel Lane at Bentley to apprise him of the situation and ask him to take care of the horses. The messenger brought word that Lane would certainly take in the horses of this eminent person who was connected to the king. Therefore, he proposed a rendezvous point known to them both from where Whitgreave could take him in when it was safe to meet Wilmot. This time the midnight rendezvous, in a wooded area at the back of Moseley Old Hall, went smoothly. Whitgreave took Lane directly to the room where Wilmot was secreted and it was only at around this time that he discovered the identity of the person he had been aiding because the colonel immediately recognised Wilmot, having served under him in the past.

Lane pointed out that because Whitgreave was a known Catholic, his home was more likely to be targeted by the authorities than his own house at Bentley and suggested that Wilmot transferred there.

Lane also offered Wilmot a means of smoothing his way to Bristol where he could slip out of England by boat. His sister Jane had only recently been granted a travel pass by the governor of Stafford, Captain Stone, allowing her to visit a relative there who was due to give birth – what if Wilmot were to accompany her, disguised as her servant? Wilmot was happy with Whitgreave's hiding places and declined the offer for the present but told Lane to hold the plan in abeyance in case a change in circumstances made it more tempting.

*

Rain was falling heavily when 'Trusty Richard' as Richard Penderel was known, led Charles out of the gatehouse, beyond the walled garden of White Ladies, and along the lanes to Spring Coppice, about half a mile to the east as the crow flies. Charles told Richard he wanted to be close enough to maintain a surveillance of the main road from his place of concealment; he preferred to be able to observe who was out in search of him, how many there were and in which direction they were headed. They chose one of the biggest trees they could find to shelter under, and it wasn't long before a band of horsemen did indeed pass by – Charles assessed them to be local militia rather than part of Cromwell's army from Worcester.

Once Charles was settled, and while brothers Humphry and George were out roving and keeping watch for any local activity, Richard left him alone for a time in order to make the short trip to the farmhouse of his sister-in-law, Margaret Yates, to request some provisions. He returned with a blanket to keep Charles dry, and soon Margaret herself appeared bearing a posset of buttered eggs, milk and sugar in a black clay cup.

'Can you,' Charles asked her, 'be faithful to a distressed Cavalier?'

'Yes, sir. I will die rather than discover you.'

Richard Penderel now stayed quietly chatting by His Majesty's side for most of the day, partaking of the posset that Charles shared with him, while looking and listening for any signs of roaming Parliamentary search parties. At one point, Charles gently interrogated him as to any local gentlemen he was aware of who might guide him and travel with him to London. Richard said that unfortunately he did not. After dwelling on this, Charles came up with a new plan. Might he, Charles asked Richard, be able to guide him westwards instead? Could he navigate a route to a crossing of the Severn so he could get into Wales and from there get on board one of the merchant vessels that traded with France? This, Trusty Richard assured him, he would be able to do. They decided to set off as soon as it got dark – but before getting onto the way proper, there was to be one last port of call. It was only two or three miles away, and it was to the west of them anyway, so in the general direction they would be travelling to reach Wales. With the enemy all around them, Richard and Charles wanted to put some finishing touches to the latter's disguise.

Later, Richard and Margaret, having noted Charles' regal bearing and diction, did what they could to train him to walk in a less upright, more casual way and to adopt as much of a rustic accent as he could manage.

*

At just after five in the afternoon, Jane, Widow Penderel of Hobbal Grange, heard the door of her farmhouse open, and was greeted by Richard, the son who lived with her there. His clothes were wet from the rain, and with him were her other sons George and Humphry, as well as Francis Yates – and one person she didn't recognise. He was equally damp, a tall slim young man with raggedly cut short hair. The identity of the visitor and what they had planned was soon explained to her, and she quickly rustled up a meal of bacon and eggs for her important guest. He ate it with Jane's granddaughter Nan perched on his knee. Charles asked his constant companion of the day, Richard, whether he would like some of his food:

'Yes, sir, I will.'

'You have a better stomach than I,' teased Charles, 'for you have eaten five times today already.'

After the meal, Jane approached the king and expressed her thanks that God had given her family the opportunity to play such an important role in keeping him safe. Then, the brothers helped prepare Charles for the next stage of his trek. From now on, His Majesty was Will Jones, a woodman arrived in the district in search of employment, and he would be carrying as his badge of office one of Richard's wood-bills – an implement used for lopping the branches of trees. Francis Yates had brought a sizeable amount of money with him and offered the king thirty shillings, of which, worried about how suspicious it might look if a woodsman were found to be carrying large amounts of cash, Charles took ten. By nine o'clock on Thursday, 4 September it was well dark outside, and all was ready. Humphry was prepared to scout ahead to make sure the coast was clear, but Charles didn't want him to put himself in any further danger and declined the offer. Jane Penderel watched as her son and his important charge passed through the door and were swallowed by the night.

*

John Penderel arrived at Boscobel, having made the nine mile cross-country trek through the night only to discover that he was too late – Charles was already heading west, for Wales. John wearily turned about to retrace his steps to inform Lord Wilmot at Moseley.

Commentary:

- There were five Penderel brothers living within close proximity of one another at this time (and a sixth probably out of the country) all fully aware of Charles' identity from the outset and all involved in helping the king in one way or another. These brothers were true countrymen, working on the land, in the woods, acting as live-in caretakers; Humphry was a miller. William, the eldest, lived at Boscobel, and John at White Ladies.

- After parting from the king, Talbot, Derby, and all other lords and senior officers (a party of about forty) struck off to the north in an attempt to meet up with General Leslie, who still commanded the remaining Scottish horse. After fighting off one attack they were eventually overpowered near Newport, around thirty miles from Worcester. Derby was court-martialled and hanged as a traitor in Bolton. Charles Giffard, who had served under Colonel Careless and whose servant Francis Yates is mentioned above, was caught at the same time as Derby but escaped. The earls of Lauderdale, Cleveland and others were taken to Tower and then Windsor Castle – remaining captive for several years. The Duke of Buckingham opted for the road Charles would soon take and adopted the disguise of a farm labourer, eventually making his way to France via London. One of Charles' retainers, Hugh May, lived in a haystack for three weeks, supported by a loyal farmer while Parliamentary soldiers were quartered in his own house. Lord Talbot took refuge at his own father's home, but because it was an obvious target he had to hide in an airless outhouse, where he ran the risk of suffocation and starvation because the constant presence of searchers meant that food couldn't be brought for him and he couldn't come out for air. Only a nocturnal visit by a servant saved him. Derby gave himself up to a Captain Edge and was tried for treason at Chester after being given a guarantee that his surrender would ensure he avoided the death sentence. However, the promise of clemency was ignored and James Stanley, 7th Earl of Derby, was taken to Bolton and beheaded in the market place. The wounded Massie gave himself up to Lady Stamford and was handed over to the authorities, but eventually escaped. Leslie himself was caught near Rochdale and imprisoned till after the Restoration.

- It is said that the Penderels surreptitiously dug a hole to hide Charles' clothes, and left them there for several weeks before recovering them.
- Edward Martin petitioned Charles after the Restoration, reminding him, in case his memory needed jolting after all that had happened to him, of the 'noggen' shirt he had provided as part of Charles' woodsman's disguise.

Chapter 6

Madeley

So that night, as soon as it was dark, Richard Penderell and I took our journey on foot towards the Severn… We came by a mill where I heard some people talking, and as we conceived it was about twelve or one o'clock at night, and the country-fellow desired me not to answer if any body should ask me any questions, because I had not the accent of the country. Just as we came to the mill, we could see the miller…sitting at the mill door, he being in white cloaths, it being a very dark night... We fell a running, both of us, up the lane, as long as we could run, it being very deep, and very dirty, till at last I bade him leap over a hedge, and lye still to hear if any body followed us; which we did, and continued lying down upon the ground about half an hour, when, hearing nobody come, we continued our way on to the village upon the Severn; where the fellow told me there was an honest gentleman... where I might be with great safety; for that he had hiding-holes for priests... But I would not go in till I knew a little of his mind, whether he would receive so dangerous a guest as me? and therefore stayed in a field, under a hedge, by a great tree, commanding him not to say it was I; but only to ask Mr Woolfe, whether he would receive an English gentleman... to hide him the next day, till we could travel again by night, for I durst not go but by night.

So I came into the house a back way, where I found Mr Woolfe, an old gentleman… And as soon as ever it began to be a little darkish, Mr Woolfe and his son brought us meat into the barn; and there we discoursed with them, whether we might safely get over the Severn into Wales; which they advised me by no means to adventure upon, because of the strict guards that were kept all along the Severn, where any passage could be found, for preventing any body's escaping that way into Wales.

Upon this I took resolution of going that night the very same way back again to Penderells house, where I knew I should hear some news, what was become of my Lord Wilmot, and resolved again upon going for London. So we set out as soon as it was dark. But, as we came by the mill again, we had no mind to be questioned a second time there; and therefore asking Richard Penderell, whether he could swim or no? and how deep the river was? He told me, it was a scurvy river, not easy to be past in all places, and that he could not swim. So I told him, that the river being but a little one, I would undertake to help him over. Upon which we went over some closes to the riverside, and I entering the river first, to see whether I could myself go over, who knew how to swim, found it was but a little above my middle; and thereupon taking Richard Penderell by the hand I helped him over.

King Charles, as dictated to Samuel Pepys

Charles' ultimate goal was Wales, but the first stop along the way was to be Madeley, a few miles south of Telford. From White Ladies the journey was around nine miles, but Charles had had very little rest since fighting for his life in a major battle and Trusty Richard discovered that it was beginning to catch up with his companion. Richard found himself having to coax and cajole the young royal into not letting up, no matter how bad he felt. So exhausted was Charles by now, having spent so long without proper sleep and having eaten only small, irregular meals, that on several occasions he sank to the ground and declared that he could go no further without a rest. He would spend the night on the spot, whatever the risk. It didn't help that the shoes he had been given didn't fit well and were causing him so much pain that he chose to take them off and walk in stockinged feet. Nevertheless, Richard Penderel, a man hardened to the outdoor life and more than twice Charles' age, resorted to a little psychology in order to keep his demoralised companion going, at times telling him the road would soon get easier, and at others, like a modern father taking his agitated children on holiday, reassuring him that they were nearly there. It worked, and Charles was somehow able to keep putting one throbbing and weary foot in front of the other through the night.

*

The miller of Evelith in the parish of Shifnal, about two miles from Madeley, was sitting in the doorway of his mill when he heard the sound of a gate closing in the darkness somewhere nearby. He was already on high alert so late at night because he was sheltering some Royalist officers and he jumped to his feet to investigate.

'Who goes there?'

'Just neighbours going home,' came a disembodied voice from out of the gloom.

'If you be neighbours, stand or I will knock you down,' the miller barked.

Instead, he heard an urgent whisper, quickly followed by the sound of two lots of footsteps scurrying away into the night.

'*Rogues! Rogues!*' the miller cried, upon which some of the soldiers spilled out of the mill and began to run in the direction the fleeing men seemed to be taking. The last the miller heard of the interlopers was a panicked splashing sound, indicating that they were escaping across the nearby Wesley Brook.

*

After urging his charge to stick close, Richard Penderel had set off at a run up a deep and muddy lane. In his haste he nearly left the struggling king behind, but the rustling of his calfskin breeches had enabled his young companion to follow in the darkness. Eventually, at Charles' behest, they vaulted a hedge and threw themselves down, listening for sounds that indicated they were still being pursued. When nothing was heard after half an hour, they felt satisfied that the chase had been abandoned, and Richard led on, taking a route through the sleeping village of Kemberton and on to Madeley. It was around midnight by the time they came to a reasonable sized Tudor mansion whose inhabitants Richard knew and felt he could trust. Charles wasn't so sure and insisted that Penderel sound out the inhabitants before he would show his face. Thus, leaving his charge hiding beneath another hedge, Trusty Richard approached the house and knocked at the door.

*

Francis Wolfe was woken from his slumbers by a knocking at the door that stirred the whole household, which consisted of his wife Mary, his four sons, and Ann, his daughter. She it was who the 69-year-old merchant sent to find out who the midnight caller might be. It emerged that the man was known to her father – but the reason for his nocturnal visit came as a shock. When Francis went to see what it was all about, Richard Penderel reported that he had someone with him – an English gentleman 'of quality' who had managed to escape the recent Battle of Worcester. Was Mr Wolfe prepared to provide him with refuge until the following night?

Francis was in a quandary. He was a Catholic and a Royalist, but the area was swarming with Parliamentary troops and the penalty for anyone caught sheltering a senior Royalist officer was bound to be death. He just couldn't risk it – at least, not for anyone other than the king himself... Now came Francis Wolfe's second shock of the night – the gentleman of quality *was* the king. All Wolfe's reservations dissipated upon hearing this, and he told Richard that he would take any risk if it meant preserving His Majesty.

Penderel soon returned with his travelling companion and Wolfe quickly apprised him of the situation locally; the militia were out in force in Madeley itself, and they had mounted a guard at the ferry. Then Wolfe explained that his being a Catholic family, the house had concealed hiding places where the king might ordinarily hide, but that previous searches for priests by the authorities had uncovered the locations of these places. Should anyone come hunting for the fleeing king, these would probably be the first places they would look. The only realistic option was his barn and so, after a hasty meal of cold meat, Wolfe had the two visitors taken across the courtyard to the timber building, where they were left in a corner, hiding behind a pile of hay. They remained there the following day, till Wolfe's son returned home after having been held a prisoner in Shrewsbury. He had observed that it was not just the ferry that was being guarded, there were lookouts all along the banks of the Severn locally. Wolfe accompanied his son to the barn with more food and this latest intelligence. On hearing this, Charles abandoned the whole idea of reaching Wales and determined to retrace his steps to the Penderels' territory around Boscobel, where as well as hoping that he might find out what had become of Lord Wilmot, he would go back to his previous plan of striking south for London. Wolfe provided Charles with more money, and his wife Mary, deciding that Charles still didn't look the part of an outdoorsman, stained his hands and face with a mixture made from boiled walnut leaves.

On the night of Friday, 5 September, Richard and Charles set off back the way they had come, guided by Wolfe's maid for the first mile or two.

*

On one of his several gruelling trips between Boscobel and Wilmot during this period, John Penderel came back to Moseley to let the earl know that Charles had made his move – he was striking out west for Wales in the company of brother Richard. With the King hopefully safely away, Wilmot now needed to decide what course he should take himself. As for John, there was nothing left for him but to return home now that Charles had left the Penderel territory.

*

Once Wolfe's maid had left them on the right path, Trusty Richard guided Charles on a weary trudge through the night once again until they reached the vicinity of Evelith Mill and its belligerent miller. Charles understandably wanted to avoid another confrontation – the problem was, his plan was to cross the river and Richard knew that it was treacherous in places. Furthermore, he had to admit to His Majesty, he couldn't swim...

Fortunately, Charles could. He offered to go into the water first to test the depth and help Richard across if need be. So it was that they veered away from the mill and crossed several fields till they came to the river bank. After finding a suitable place, Richard looked on in the gloom as his king lowered himself into the chilly waters. Reassured by his companion that the water only came up to his waist, Richard grasped Charles' outstretched hand and allowed himself to be helped to the other side. They clambered out and squelched off in the general direction of Boscobel.

Commentary:

- Some accounts name the fearsome miller at Evelith as Roger Bushell, but the sole source for this seems to be from a novel, albeit a historically very accurate one, by the Victorian writer William Francis Ainsworth (*Boscobel the Royal Oak: a Tale of the Year 1651*).
- The 'river' (the word comes from Charles' own recollection) referred to on their return trip can only have been the Wesley Brook, which would present little obstacle now but which was almost certainly much deeper in the seventeenth century.
- The Wolfe family were later offered an annuity, but being well-off graciously declined this assistance. Their only request was for augmentation of their arms: an imperial crown was added to their crest of a demi-wolf in 1661.

Chapter 7

Return to Boscobel

We went on our way to one of Penderell's brothers… When I came to this house, I inquired where my Lord Wilmot was; it being now towards morning, and having travelled these two nights on foot… Penderell's brother told me, that he had conducted him to a very honest gentleman's house, one Mr Pitchcroft... [Whitgreave] a Roman Catholic. I asked him, what news? He told me, that there was one Major Careless in the house that was that country-man; whom I knowing, he having been a major in our army… He told me, that it would be very dangerous for me either to stay in that house, or to go into the wood, there being a great wood hard by Boscobel; that he knew but one way how to pass the next day, and that was, to get up into a great oak, in a pretty plain place, where we might see round about us; for the enemy would certainly search at the wood for people that had made their escape. [They] got up into a great oak, that had been lopt some three or four years before, and being grown out again, very bushy and thick, could not be seen through, and here we staid all the day...

Memorandum, That while we were in this tree we see soldiers going up and down, in the thicket of the wood, searching for persons escaped, we seeing them, now and then, peeping out of the wood.

King Charles, as dictated to Samuel Pepys

It was early on the morning of Saturday, 6 September, three days after the Battle of Worcester, when Joan Penderel was alerted to a commotion at the door. She and her husband William, eldest of the Penderels, were the housekeepers of Boscobel House, a hunting lodge set in a thickly wooded area on the White Ladies Estate. It was owned by Charles Giffard, who had converted and extended the century-old farmhouse to suit his own purposes.

CHARLES II AND HIS ESCAPE INTO EXILE

Joan was aware of the secret venture her husband and brothers-in-law had become entangled in these last couple of days, but she was surprised to see Richard return not only so soon, but with the king still in tow. Wasn't her husband supposed to have guided his valuable travelling companion across the Severn to safety in Wales?

Once the situation had been explained to her, Charles was particularly keen to find out what news they had of Lord Wilmot. Joan hadn't heard from anyone of that name – there was, however, a Catholic gentleman called Careless in the house right at that moment. Charles immediately realised that this must be Major William Careless, one of his officers who had courageously led charges through the streets of Worcester to give him a little extra time in which to make his escape. Charles told her that he was very eager to see her visitor.

*

After fighting his way through Worcester's narrow streets to buy Charles time, Colonel William Careless had used his local knowledge to make his way to the secluded cottage of one David Jones on Tong Heath. He had been lying low there for two days, when news was brought to him that Charles was being sheltered just a few miles away at White Ladies. A local woman, Elizabeth Burgess, was prepared to guide him to the location.

Reunited with the young man he had risked his life to save, and seeing him foot-sore, bedraggled and weary but still alive, Careless couldn't prevent the tears from streaming down face and Charles himself reacted in kind. Joan Penderel served them some bread and cheese and made them a posset of milk and small beer. While she was heating water to wash His Majesty's feet, Careless tugged Charles' sodden, ill-fitting and much-hated boots off and emptied them of the gravel and other debris that had collected in them along the way. Joan saw that his feet were in shreds and it was clear that the poor man could barely walk. She immediately began tending to her patient, peeling off his tattered stockings, paring away the blistered skin from his feet and gently bathing them.

Charles and Careless now needed to decide on their next step and the major, knowing from his own travels and the intelligence he had picked up that neither the house nor the surrounding area – including the woods – were currently safe, believed a new plan was needed. Careless came up with a novel solution. He told Charles of a large oak tree in the vicinity whose leaves and stout branches could successfully hide him from pursuers. Autumn was still a little way off and the tree was still in full leaf, so Charles

38

was happy to accept this plan and allow Careless to show him the way. The natural platform at the top of the trunk, where the previously pollarded branches spread out, was some way off the ground, so William Penderel accompanied them with a ladder. It was perfect, in as much as they were hidden from view from below but had a great vantage point from which to see anyone who might be approaching. Sure enough, it wasn't long before they began to spot soldiers on the ground searching the area, flitting and out of the trees but fortunately never paying any close attention to the great oak.

*

In the meantime, Humphry Penderel, the miller among the brothers, had a journey of his own to make. Ostensibly, it was a routine one that had nothing to do with Charles or the recent battle, but it served the dual purpose of a scouting mission to see what was happening in the region. He made the three mile trip to Shifnal, and the house of Captain Broadway (a heel-maker in normal times, but a Parliamentary army captain during the current crisis) to whom he was obliged to pay twenty shillings in taxes towards the costs of the local militia. It just so happened that while Humphry was in Broadway's house going about his business, a Parliamentary colonel, newly arrived from the fighting at Worcester, turned up asking the captain whether nearby White Ladies had been included in the checks for the whereabouts of the king, since he had heard rumours that Charles Stuart had been there.

Penderel must have struggled to remain expressionless while listening to Broadway, replying that he knew nothing beyond rumour – but adding that the colonel was in luck, because the man with him was a miller whose brother just happened to be the caretaker there. After fending off the officer's initial questions, Humphry eventually conceded that the stories of Charles having visited were true but spun a yarn that it was highly unlikely that he could stay there since there were already three families living at White Ladies, and they themselves were all at loggerheads with each other. Perhaps suspecting this to be the disingenuous story it actually was, the colonel dangled the prospect of a £1,000 reward under Humphry's nose, while darkly making it clear that Charles was expected to be caught very soon and anyone known to have aided him could expect to meet a gruesome end.

*

During the day, while Charles and Careless were hiding in the tree, Richard Penderel made a trip to Wolverhampton, seven miles or more away. The more mundane part of his mission was to restock Boscobel with provisions for the king and the others, but there was an ulterior motive. While there, he sought out a trusted man called George Mainwaring to see if he knew of a place where two refugees from the Battle of Worcester might be safely concealed for a time. Mainwaring himself had nothing to offer, but he did know of someone in Moseley, not too far off, who might. His name was Whitgreave. Trusty Richard made a mental note of this for his return trip – unaware that Charles' roaming companion Lord Wilmot was already with Whitgreave.

*

Back in the oak tree, Careless and Charles had a couple of pillows provided by William Penderel to make them more comfortable, and Careless was soon to discover to his cost just how comfortable, since, while William and his wife Elizabeth prowled the general area under the pretence of gathering firewood, the exhausted Charles fell asleep leaning against his companion. At first the colonel was happy to support his king, but as time went on, he began to experience painful cramping and pins and needles till he could barely tolerate it. Reluctant though he was to wake the king, whom he knew must be in dire need of rest, he eventually felt obliged to give him a little pinch in order to alert him to their precarious situation. At least Careless was able to make up somewhat for rousing the king by producing a snack of bread and cheese with some small beer to wash it down, something that Joan had handed to him before they had taken up their position. Other provisions were hoisted up by the Penderels when the coast was clear using a long stick.

*

When Humphry Penderel returned to White Ladies with news of the enormous reward being offered for his capture, Charles, now back at the house from his arboreal hideout and in fact sitting in the garden drinking wine that Richard had bought back from his trip to Wolverhampton, was dismayed, knowing that such an amount would mean he could live in comfort for many years if not the rest of his life. But Humphry was quick to join Careless in assuring him that no amount of money could tempt them to betray their rightful sovereign.

Feeling suitably reassured, Charles now informed the Penderels that he felt it was time to prepare for the next leg of his journey.

William was asked by the king to shave his whiskers and attend to his hair once more to try to cut it 'according to the country mode' in order to enhance his disguise and his Will Jones persona. Hairdressing wasn't

40

quite William's forte; he did his best, clipping it as short as the scissors would allow on top but leaving more length at the sides as befitted the look they wanted.

'Will is but a mean barber,' Colonel Careless joked on seeing the results of William Penderel's handiwork.

Charles knew that in view of the kind of appearance he was seeking, this was probably a bonus. 'I have never been shaved by a barber before,' he replied drily. He then, wishing to dispose of even the tiniest clue of his presence here (for the Penderels' sake as well as his own) Charles asked Will to burn the hair clippings. Will assented, gathering up the black locks and taking them away. In fact, once out of sight of Charles and Careless he destroyed some but surreptitiously saved enough to make a memento of his illustrious visitor and the historic role his family was playing in this drama.

*

Joan Penderel must have been glowing inside somewhat as she prepared chicken for one of Charles' final meals with them before departing, since he had referred to her as 'My dame Joan'. Once they had eaten, it was decided to risk one of White Ladies' priest-holes just for this one night. Joan's husband and some of his brothers kept up a night watch around the perimeter of the house, along with the roads and paths in the vicinity. The hidey-hole, accessed by a trapdoor concealing a narrow opening in the floor of one of the smaller rooms, was built for secrecy not comfort, and the six-foot-two Charles spent a fitful night there.

*

When the morning of Sunday, 7 September arrived, Charles was able to feast on mutton. William Penderel had seen to this by 'acquiring' and slaughtering a sheep from the fields of one of the Boscobel tenants. He enjoyed what was, in his present circumstances, a relative feast, after spending some time upstairs at prayer as well as gazing out at the road between Tong and Brewood. When Charles had come down to join them for the meal, Will and the others noticed that his nose had suddenly started bleeding, causing some concern that he might be ill. However, he reassured them that he was prone to such bouts and was used to them, so Will fell to cutting up the sheep, taking a leg for the king.

Charles cut a few 'collops' from it and, requesting a pan and butter, took it upon himself to perform the frying duties. There arose a light-hearted debate as to who out of Will Penderel and Charles was the cook and who the scullion, or menial kitchen servant. Since no one could agree, the king himself was asked to adjudicate – and declared that he was both.

When John Penderel turned up, he was taken aback to see Charles at Boscobel once more. Upon informing the king that Lord Wilmot was being hidden by Mr Whitgreave at Moseley, Charles, fearing to stay in this area any longer, decided that his best option would be to join the earl. So it was that yet again the doughty John was on the road – this time to let Wilmot know of Charles' latest intentions.

*

Whitgreave and Huddleston were walking in the orchard in the grounds of Moseley Old Hall, discussing riding over to White Ladies to find out what was happening, when they encountered a very worried looking John Penderel who wanted to know where Lord Wilmot was. They explained that he had already left them for Colonel Lane at Bentley.

'Then we are all undone,' said Penderel, who told them the story of Charles' return to Boscobel, how the area was alive with searchers and the king had been desperate enough to hide in a tree. After a short discussion, Whitgreave and Huddleston decided that the situation could be saved. The best plan was for Wilmot to be recalled to Moseley, and the king be somehow smuggled here himself so that they could be reunited and see what might be done from there.

*

Whitgreave, Huddleston and John Penderel hurried over to see Colonel Lane, where Whitgreave informed him that Penderel had been sent by 'some person of eminent quality whose name he was not to discover' but who wished to be taken to Lord Wilmot. Lane showed John to the earl and he returned with the news that Wilmot wished to rejoin the king that night. He sent the three visitors back to Moseley, with a plan for himself to follow them that evening and meet them at the wooded spot in his grounds where Lane had met Whitgreave before. John Penderel was sent yet again to Boscobel to tell the king of the plan and arrange for him and his brothers bring Charles to Moseley some time after Wilmot was scheduled to arrive.

*

Later that afternoon, John arrived back at Boscobel with the news of Wilmot's proposal and it was decided that Charles would set out at eleven that same night. The only problem was that, despite his restful couple of days here, his shredded feet hadn't recovered sufficiently for him to be confident of being able to walk such a distance. John was therefore sent to procure a horse from a neighbour, only to find when he got there that it had already been loaned out to someone else. Plan B was for him to borrow Humphry Penderel's big old nag. This he duly did, and it was soon saddled and ready for the journey.

With the preparations in place, Charles was summoned. He wanted both John and Careless to go with him, but the colonel feared that as a local man, well known in the districts they would be travelling in, he would be a liability to the king. Charles reluctantly accepted this argument; but now John Penderel, backed by Careless, expressed their reservations about how safe it was for just the two of them to be travelling abroad. Again, Charles saw the wisdom in this argument and so it was that the company which departed Boscobel that night consisted of (in addition to Charles) John Penderel himself, his brothers Humphry, William, Richard and George; and Francis Yates, the Penderels' brother-in-law. All were armed – some with pistols, all with bill-hooks or pikestaffs. In travelling, by necessity, as such brazenly armed gang, there could be no pretence that this was merely an innocent journey abroad should they meet anyone along the way. If they were challenged, they would have to stand and fight. The party formed a sort of phalanx around the king: two went ahead; two flanked his horse; and the remaining pair hung well back so that they could hold off any attackers approaching from their rear and perhaps give the king time to escape. With Humphry holding his horse's bridle, he led the king out of the gates of Boscobel and off along the highway just as the light began to fade.

Commentary:

- At that time Boscobel was owned by Frances Giffard, widow of John Cotton (not the Charles Giffard who accompanied the royal party, as is often stated), but she wasn't at the house when these events took place.
- Some accounts say the famous oak was hollow, but Allan Fea (in *Flight of the King*) pours scorn on this. The tree, he says, had a small hole 'about the bigness of a man's hand' in the trunk, which has led to the exaggerated stories of its hollowness. Boscobel and the 'royal' oak became popular tourist attractions even during Charles' lifetime, but for that very reason the tree itself did not fare as well as the man it had protected. Writing in 1660, Thomas Blount (*Boscobel*) said that within a short time of the Restoration and

subsequent stories of Charles' adventures, which quickly elevated the tree to celebrity status, 'hundreds of people for many miles around' flocked to visit the spot. The unfortunate consequence of this that the tree was 'depriv'd of all its young boughs' as souvenirs. Four years later the diarist John Evelyn, in his book *Sylva*, reported that so many people had cut away branches and even bark from the noble oak which had been so well tended by the Penderels, that it had been killed off. Dr Charlet, writing to Samuel Pepys in 1702 informs him that the tree is now enclosed within a circular wall, by which time Allan Fea says that just the trunk remained, and that split in two. By 1713 the antiquary Dr Stukely recorded the tree as having been 'almost cut away' - but that a sapling from one of its acorns was now growing beside it. We don't hear of it again for nearly two hundred years, when a traveller was told by locals that the remaining stump and roots had been dug up 'many years ago'. The 'new' Royal Oak can still be seen today, since it and Boscobel House are owned by English Heritage. Oak Apple Day was commemorated for many years afterwards, and still is in certain parts of England (see Chapter 21).

- Lady Wood, who claimed to have heard Charles telling the story of his escape, has him estimating the oak to have been ten or twelve yards from the road. She also claims that Careless 'quaked and shak't' so much that Charles feared the shaking of the leaves it caused would give them away. This doesn't sound like Careless, however, a brave military veteran, and is probably an exaggeration for effect or levity (either by Lady Wood or Charles himself).

- William Penderel did attempt to make amends for taking the sheep that fed Charles, as Blunt tells us: 'The danger being over, honest William began to think of making satisfaction for the fat mutton, and accordingly tendered Mr Staunton its worth in money; but Staunton, understanding the sheep was killed for the relief of some honest Cavaliers, refused to take the money, but wished, much good might it do them.'

- Some time after the king had departed Boscobel for the last time, Colonel Careless sent Will Penderel to Wolverhampton for a meeting with his friend Humphrey Ironmonger. Ironmonger managed to inveigle a travel pass from the Parliamentary authorities, made out in a false name which Careless adopted and used to escape to France, and from there to Holland.

Chapter 8

Moseley

That night Richard Penderell and I went to Mr Pitchcroft's [Whitgreave's]... Here I spoke with my Lord Wilmot, and sent him away to Colonel Lane's...to see what means could be found for my escaping towards London; who told my Lord, after some consultation thereon, that he had a sister that had a very fair pretence of going hard by Bristol, to a cousin of hers that was married to one Mr Norton, who lived two or three miles towards Bristol...and she might carry me thither as her man; and from Bristol I might find shipping to get out of England... I went away to Colonel Lane's, where I changed my cloaths.

King Charles, as dictated to Samuel Pepys

Humphry Penderel, leading the king on his big old mill horse through the lanes to the south west, found the journey mercifully uneventful compared to the trials his brother Trusty Richard had endured during the abortive attempt to cross the Severn. The only attack came from the king himself, albeit a light-hearted one.

'This is the heaviest dull jade I ever rode on,' Charles wryly remarked.

Humphry wasn't too deferential to refrain from defending his faithful beast. 'My liege – can you blame the horse to go heavily when he has the weight of three kingdoms on his back?'

There was one river to cross along the route (the Penk), and a couple of miles further on they reached Pendleford Old Mill. Here, Humphry was relieved of his duties, since it was decided it would be safer and attract less attention if the last leg of the journey was made on foot. Consequently, once Charles had dismounted, Humphry turned the horse about and he, William and George Penderel began to retrace their steps back to Boscobel having performed their brave and loyal services to the king. But before they had got very far, Humphry heard Charles calling after them.

'My troubles make me forget myself,' he said approaching them. 'I thank you all.'

They kissed his hand and then, partings over, the remaining Penderels – Richard and John – along with Francis Yates, trudged with Charles across several rain-sodden fields to a pre-arranged meeting place in a grove of trees on Whitgreave's land.

*

Thomas Whitgreave and John Huddleston, having made sure the occupants of the house were in bed, waited anxiously for the expected arrivals, Whitgreave at the out-of-the-way spot, known as Alport's Leasow ('leasow' being an archaic term for a type of pasture field) to meet Wilmot, and Huddleston in an orchard elsewhere in the estate. Wilmot appeared on time and Whitgreave took him into the house, but when the king's scheduled arrival time passed, Wilmot sent him out to look for Huddleston to find out what was happening. Huddleston was still waiting – there was no sign of Charles.

Wilmot feared the worst when he heard this. Every passing minute increased the probability that the king had been captured by prowling soldiers or militia, and he asked Whitgreave to go back out and wait with Huddleston. This time, he didn't have to wait too long before seeing the small group of shadowy figures approaching. Wilmot was waiting at the door with a lantern to guide their way. At first, Whitgreave couldn't distinguish Charles from the rest. This time, he was wearing a white 'steeple-crowned' hat lined with grease, a dirty and tattered leather doublet, an equally shabby green woodsman's coat partly kept in one piece by an assortment of patches, matching breeches with loose flaps dangling from the waist to the knees, and much-darned grey stockings. The outfit was finished off by a pair of patched-up shoes with splits in the uppers which let in the rain, and in his hand, he carried a misshapen thorn walk stick. Whitgreave did know the Penderels, however, so as his eyes adjusted to the light he was able to work out who the king was by a process of elimination. He took Charles to his room, then came down and led the doughty Penderel brothers to the buttery so they could get something to eat and drink.

When Whitgreave returned he found Huddleston, who had been sent by the king to invite him up.

When he got to Charles' room, Wilmot, who was with him, said, 'This gentlemen whom you see under this disguise, whom I have hitherto concealed, is both your master and mine and, and the master to whom we all owe our duty and allegiance.'

Whitgreave and Huddleston knelt as Charles stepped forward and offered them his hand to kiss in the traditional manner. Then the king asked them to rise, telling them how strongly Wilmot had vouched for their character and loyalty. Charles was well aware that they had been, and were, prepared help him and his friends in their hour of need, and that their support would never be forgotten. But it wasn't long before Charles' thoughts turned to more practical matters, wanting to know about the hiding place he had been told of. Without delay, Whitgreave took the king up a broad oak staircase, across a wainscoted bedroom in which there was a made-up bed, a chair, and a fireplace in which a previously prepared fire sent out its warm orange glow into the room. Whitgreave led Charles over to a built-in cupboard, within which, by pressing the panelling in the right place, he caused a small concealed door to open – thus revealing the priest-hole.

Charles wanted to try it out for size and having done so declared himself satisfied. Before long, though, Charles experienced another nosebleed, and once more reassured his hosts that he was prone to them and it was nothing to worry about. When Charles produced the rough piece of rag given to him by the Penderels for a handkerchief in order to staunch the flow of blood, it was the turn of Whitgreave's priest, Huddleston, to step forward with a much finer item for the king to use.

They retired to the main bedroom of the house, which had been assigned to Charles for the duration of his stay. The weary king slumped into a chair by the fire and stretched his legs out so that Whitgreave and Huddleston could peel off his worn-out shoes and the paper with which they had been lined in a vain attempt to make them fit better. Then they pulled off the filthy stockings and washed his aching, blistered feet. Charles now divested himself of his other rough clothes and replaced them with rather better quality apparel belonging to both Whitgreave and Huddleston. Whitgreave then produced a snack of 'biscuit bread' (possibly a form of shortbread) and sack (fortified white Spanish wine), and the refreshment restored Charles' spirits.

'I am now ready for another march; and if it shall please God once more to place me in the head of but eight or ten thousand good men, of one mind, and resolved to fight, I shall not doubt to drive these rogues out of my kingdoms.'

*

Whitgreave and Huddleston now withdrew to allow Charles to talk privately into the night with Lord Wilmot about their next move. By the time they had finished it was around five in the morning, and Charles was left to try to get some sleep.

The next day, Monday, 8 September, Whitgreave spun a story for his staff that Huddleston was temporarily giving refuge to a Cavalier acquaintance escaping from Worcester (technically perfectly true) and found excuses to send his servants on errands which would keep them out of the way; the one person he kept on hand to tend to his special guests' needs was his Catholic cook-maid. Father Huddleston posted three boys under his tutelage at Moseley Hall as look-outs at the upper windows. The only person in the house who was told the full facts about Charles was Whitgreave's mother, and when she took him a meal, he asked her to sit and talk with him for a while.

Huddleston spent most of Monday ensconced with the king in his room, listening as Charles gave him an account of what had happened at Worcester. To maintain secrecy, they ate together there and Whitgreave himself carried the food from below stairs rather than trust a servant; his mother was brought in to carve the meat. Charles was keen to get a sense of how much support he had at large, and to that end Whitgreave was sent on a reconnaissance mission to Wolverhampton and to arrange for Colonel Lane to bring Wilmot's horses to transport Charles on his journey to Bentley.

*

The following day, Charles, still staying out of sight but seeing Whitgreave's study door open, wanted to explore inside with the host and Huddleston for a change of scenery. The study window gave a view down onto Moseley's main street and Charles was pained to see more stragglers of his once proud army – some of whom he actually recognised – making their slow and painful way to whatever place of safety they could as best they could. Many of them would have been Scots, a long way from home and no doubt dreaming of the day when they would see their own families once more. It was a sorry sight. Some snatched up scraps of food in the street thrown out by householders, some knocked on doors begging for food or first aid. Moseley Hall was no exception and old Mrs Whitgreave herself tended to the wounded men who dared to call as tenderly as she had assisted the king. One man who came to the house that day assured Mrs Whitgreave that after retreating from Worcester, Charles had been joined by three other kings at Warrington Bridge, where he had inflicted a defeat on his enemy. When she told Charles about this, he replied wistfully that 'Surely they are the three kings of heaven, for I can imagine none else.'

*

Parliamentarian Colonel Edward Ashenhurst and the men of his militia had been exercising their persuasive powers on a soldier captured fleeing Worcester, trying to extract from him the last known whereabouts of the elusive Charles. And now, he led his men to White Ladies. When the Parliamentarians battered on the door and were met by Humphry Penderel, they demanded to know what the inhabitants had done with 'Charles Stuart'. Penderel complained that a group of passing Cavaliers had invaded his home and eaten his all of food – but he didn't know who they were nor where they went next. Next, the militia sent for the owner, George Giffard, who told the same story even when a pistol was poked in his chest. Giffard merely stuck to his guns and asked if he might say a prayer before they shot him.

'If you can tell us no news you shall get no prayers,' growled one of Ashenhurst's men. But one of the officers over-ruled the threats, and the invaders withdrew to continue their search elsewhere – after venting their frustration in the form of a beating meted out on the informant, whom they accused of deliberately leading them on a wild goose chase.

*

Wilmot now rode back to Colonel Lane to arrange for him to bring the horses back the next night, to carry the king to his home at Bentley. They now planned to take advantage of the fact that Colonel Lane's sister had the perfect excuse to be travelling in the direction of a southern port (at a time when travelling abroad for any distance was forbidden without written authorization) with company. She would use her pass from the Parliamentary governor of Staffordshire to visit her cousin near Bristol, who was soon to give birth.

*

In London at just about this time, Parliament witnessed an unusual interruption to its normal business when word arrived that one Captain Orpyn was at the very door of the chamber, fresh from the Battle of Worcester seven days previously. He was admitted and presented a letter from Oliver Cromwell which declared that his emissary had in his possession royal colours (amounting to around a hundred flags), captured during the battle.

It was immediately resolved that the gallant captain be awarded £100, and that the colours should be displayed in Westminster Hall. This dramatic little interlude seemed to galvanise that day's session, since Parliament itself went on the offensive by issuing a Proclamation 'for the Discovery and Apprehending of Charles Stuart, and other Traitors, his adherents' and announced that a reward of £1,000 was on offer to that end. The Proclamation would be printed and issued to all counties and cities in the land.

*

Charles talked to Huddleston about what it was like for Catholics under the current regime, and the priest decided to take him up to see the little chapel he had created at the top of the house to view his religious books and altar. On viewing the latter item, Charles wistfully remembered back to his own crucifix and silver candlesticks, and how Lord Holland disposed of them, 'which he hath now paid for'. (The Earl of Holland was executed at around the same time as Charles' own father.) Charles was very taken with Huddleston's books, and even expressed a desire to take one with him when he moved on. When they had finished talking, Huddleston left Charles to get some rest. His nap wasn't to last long.

*

Elizabeth Smith, Mrs Whitgreave's servant, had good reason to be grateful for Charles' stay at Moseley, since after a time she and her daughter had been brought into his presence so that they might be touched by His Majesty in order to cure them of the 'evil', the skin disease scrofula – a belief and practice stemming back to the Middle Ages. But her current mission was much more urgent in nature. She bounded up the stairs crying *'Soldiers! Soldiers are coming!'*

Ignoring any sort of royal protocol, she burst into Charles' room to wake him. The caring, quick-thinking maid then found a bunch of sweet-smelling herbs, and as Charles roused himself and prepared to make for the priest-hole he'd been shown on his arrival, Elizabeth went ahead of him and scattered the aromatic plants around the floor of the hideout. There was no telling how long he would be forced to remain there, and it might make his confinement that little bit more bearable.

*

Whitgreave had been looking out of an upstairs window and had seen a neighbour coming running up to his door to bring Elizabeth the maid news of the soldiers. He decided to take the initiative. He rushed out (after first opening the doors to all the rooms as a sign that he had nothing to hide) and intercepted them before they could come to his front door – but he was met with an aggressive, hostile reception. They accused Whitgreave of having taken part in the Battle of Worcester himself, and were on the verge of arresting him. He (honestly) insisted that they were wrong – he had been ill and hadn't left his house for two weeks. At first, they refused to believe him, but when the story was verified by neighbours, they reluctantly accepted his defence and moved on without even searching his house. Whitgreave made sure they had all departed the area before going back inside to tell Charles the coast was clear.

*

While Whitgreave was being roughly interrogated by the soldiers, one of their party – Southall, 'a great priest-catcher' – approached a blacksmith shoeing horses nearby whether he had any news of the king's whereabouts, mentioning the reward of £1,000 for such information. This was where Whitgreave's need-to-know security measures probably paid off, for the smith was either unable or unwilling to pass any information to his inquisitor.

*

At around midnight on Tuesday, 9 September, Whitgreave ventured out to a corner of his orchard to fulfil a pre-arranged rendezvous with Colonel Lane, who had arrived from Bentley with the horses to escort Charles back there. Once contact had been established, Whitgreave left Lane in the orchard and went to let the king know it was time for him to move on.

Before taking his leave, Charles bade a genuinely fond farewell to Father Huddleston, Whitgreave, and his mother, and assured them he was well aware of the personal risks they had taken in sheltering him. If he was ever fortunate enough to be able to return to these shores and claim the throne, he would see to it that they were rewarded. They knelt before him and kissed his hand in parting, and while still kneeling they all prayed that God would see the king safely accomplish his mission. Whitgreave now prepared to lead Charles out into the cold night, but before he could go Mrs Whitgreave gave the king some raisins, almonds and sweetmeats for the journey, and Huddleston offered him his cloak for extra warmth. Charles, who in a short time had gained a great deal of experience of these autumnal, nocturnal expeditions, gladly accepted.

Commentary:

- While the Penderels have deservedly earned their place in history for the enormous and vital part they played in the preservation of the king, a mention here must be made of a man called Robert Bird (sometimes spelt 'Burd' and 'Beard') of Tong. Allan Fea in *The Flight of the King* draws attention to a Robert Beard who was the landlord of the Talbot inn at Tong in 1664. While rarely getting much of a mention in the story of Charles' escape, Bird seems to have acted as a sort of scout-cum-spy, gathering intelligence in the area and passing it on to the Penderels, Careless and others around the king. Presumably, word of his clandestine activities eventually came out and vengeance was brought upon on him financially if not physically, because he was 'utterly ruined' and unable support his family afterwards. After the Restoration, Giffard and Careless made sure his name was brought to the attention of Charles – who may not have even come into contact with Bird – and he was awarded a small annuity.

- Francis Yates is the only civilian who lost his life for his part in aiding Charles in his escape. He was arrested not long after bidding the king farewell, and when he refused to give any details of Charles' whereabouts he was hanged at Oxford. Charles did, however, award a pension to his widow. Note that this Francis Yates, husband of Margaret, should not be confused with the man of the same name who helped guide Charles during the first part of his journey after leaving Worcester. (Though he is – often!)

- Upon swapping the king's 'old coarse clout' for his own 'fair handkerchief' when Charles came down with a nosebleed, Father Huddleston slyly pocketed the rag soaked in the royal blood as a keepsake. He also kept the coarse shirt he took from the king after supplying him with a better one. In later life, Father Huddleston was summoned to King Charles' bedside as he lay dying so that he could convert to Roman Catholicism. The Duke of York is reported to have told Charles, 'Sire, this good man once saved your life. He now comes to save your soul.' Charles saw to it that Huddleston's cloak was later returned to its owner. (In his own account, Charles refers to Huddleston throughout as 'Hurlston', and Whitgreave as 'Mr Pitchcroft'. On this latter point he seems to be confusing the name of his helper with that of a field called Pitchcroft outside Worcester, where some of his forces were deployed.)

- The Earl of Holland, Henry Rich (mentioned above as having disposed of Charles' candlesticks and crucifix) was a courtier who fought for King Charles I in the Second Civil War, was captured at St Neots and executed. Charles' words may refer to the beginning of his father's reign, when his father gave silver candlesticks and other royal items to Holland and the Duke of Buckingham so they could be sold to raise money after Parliament had refused to grant him any more owing to his extravagant lifestyle.

- Elizabeth Smith, the maid who alerted Charles to the arrival of Cromwell's men and who spread herbs around the priest-hole to make his stay more bearable, petitioned the king for a small annuity once he was restored to the throne, reminding him that she was involved in: 'making your Majesties fire and bed in your Majesties chamber there; and particularly when your Majesty was at your repose, or rest upon your bed, and sound asleep, and notice given that Cromwell's soldiers was about the towne, etc., your Majesties petitioner rubbed softly your Majesty upon the feet and leggs to wake your Majesty, and warne your Majesty thereof, and provided sweet herbes into the private place ere your Majesty went therein, and other services did do for your Majesty…'

Chapter 9

Jane Lane

Mrs Lane and I took our journey towards Bristol, resolving to lye at a place called Long-Marson, in the vale of Esham. But we had not gone two hours on our way but the mare I rode on cast a shoe; so we were forced to ride to get another shoe at a scattering village... And as I was holding my horses foot, I asked the smith what news? He told me, that there was no news, that he knew of, since the good news of the beating of the rogues the Scots. I asked him, whether there was none of the English taken, that joined with the Scots? He answered, that he did not hear that that rogue Charles Stewart was taken; but some of the others, he said, were taken, but not Charles Stewart. I told him, that if that rogue were taken he deserved to be hanged, more than all the rest, for bringing in the Scots. Upon which he said, that I spoke like an honest man, and so we parted.

A mile before we came to Stratford upon Avon, we espied upon the way a troop of horse... Mrs Lane's sister's husband... said, that for his part he would not go by them, for he had been once or twice beaten by some of the Parliament soldiers, and he would not run the venture again. I hearing him say so, begged Mrs Lane, softly in her ear, that we might not turn back, but go on, if they should see us turn. But all she could say in the world would not do, but her brother-in-law turned quite round, and went into Stratford another way. The troop of horse being then just getting on horse-back, about twice twelve score off, and, as I told her, we did meet the troop just but in the town of Stratford.

King Charles, as dictated to Samuel Pepys

In the early hours of Tuesday, 10 September, Colonel Lane escorted Charles, on Lord Wilmot's horses, from the apple orchard south of Whitgreave's house and along the road south toward Bentley. John Lane was in his early forties, described by Lord Clarendon as being fearless, and possessing 'integrity superior to any temptation', and Bentley was his birthplace. He and his father had both been fined by Parliament for supporting Charles' father during the civil war. John had served as a cavalry officer in the conflict and was among the prisoners taken when Ashby-de-la-Zouch castle surrendered. He commanded the Walsall Royalists at the time of Worcester, but they failed to reach the battlefield in time to aid the king's cause.

Lane and Charles arrived at Bentley Hall at around midnight. The building that loomed out of the darkness as they trotted their horses towards the gate was a substantial Elizabethan manor house with steep gables, set in a deer park a few miles east of Wolverhampton. It had been thoroughly ransacked by Parliamentary soldiers in 1644. After seeing to it that his important guest had been supplied with food and drink, Colonel Lane and Wilmot, who had been waiting for him there, held talks with Charles about the next leg of his journey for a time, before they all went to get some much-needed sleep. Early the next morning, Lane provided the king with a new disguise – in fact, a new persona. He was to be transformed (and to some extent promoted) from rough woodsman Will Jones into farmer's son Will Jackson, wearing his Sunday best. To this end he was provided with a leather doublet, a grey cloth suit, and patched breeches. Lane also provided Charles with the not insignificant sum amount of £20 to cover his forthcoming expenses.

Just as it was getting light, Charles took his leave of Lord Wilmot. The earl's destination was the same as the king's, but the plan was for him to ride well apart from the group in the guise of a gentleman out hawking – he rode with a hawk on his gauntlet and was accompanied by a servant called Robert Swan. Charles pressed Wilmot to adopt some sort of proper disguise, but Wilmot complained that he would 'look frightfully' in it and flatly refused.

Colonel Lane then led the king to the stables, and while he prepared Charles' horse (one much better suited to the task ahead than Humphry Penderel's worthy but plodding brute), he provided him with some last-minute coaching concerning his new Will Jackson role. Once Charles was mounted, the colonel asked him to ride round to Bentley Hall's main gate where he would meet his 'mistress' for the forthcoming journey, his sister, Jane Lane, an attractive woman with light brown hair swept back on her head all but for a few fashionable ringlets, giving the impression of a high forehead. She was to ride behind Charles on the same horse (a not uncommon arrangement at that time), and was there waiting for him, as was her mother. She had come to see her daughter off but had no idea of the true identity of her attendant.

'Will, thou must give my sister thy hand,' Colonel Lane enjoined 'Will Jackson'. But Charles was unaccustomed to having to share his horse with anyone, let alone helping them mount up; he offered the wrong hand, causing old Mrs Lane to ask her son with amusement what kind of horseman he had engaged to ride with his sister. Once this awkwardness had been sorted out, the party set forth towards Stratford-upon-Avon.

Also in the party were Cornet Henry Lassels (who was related to Lane and had served under him during the civil war) Lane's sister Withy, and her husband John Petre. Lassels rode alone, while Withy and her husband – neither of whom had been told who Charles really was – were on the same horse. They had trekked through Rowley Regis and Quinton when, approximately two hours into this leg of the journey, the king's horse lost a shoe. This caused them to make a detour to what was then the little village of Bromsgrove. It was Charles' duty, as Jane's attendant, to take the horse to the local smith, whose forge he located at a road junction near the centre of town.

*

It was still early morning when the Bromsgrove blacksmith heard the clip-clop of an approaching horse. The young man he greeted was tall and slim, dressed in a grey cloth cloak and green breeches and appeared to be some sort of servant. He announced himself as the attendant to a lady who was travelling to Bristol to visit her sister, who was with child. This attendant, speaking in a rather strange accent, explained that their horse had lost a shoe and asked the smith if he could replace it – which he was happy to do.

'What news?' the customer casually asked as he helped by holding the horse's foot while the blacksmith worked.

The smith told the servant that he hadn't heard anything since the good news of the beating of the Scottish invaders at Worcester. As he worked with his hammer, the tall man wondered if he knew of any English prisoners from the battle in addition to those Scots who had been taken. He seemed particularly inquisitive about the late battle, but then, it had been the biggest talking point for some time so there was little unusual in that. Some were, he informed his questioner, but as far as he was aware, 'that rogue Charles Stuart' was not among them.

The servant echoed the smith's sense of aggrievement, adding that Charles Stuart was more deserving of execution than anyone else on account of being responsible for bringing the Scots across the border in the first place.

The blacksmith commended him for speaking 'like an honest man', and the attendant led his re-shod horse away to rejoin his mistress.

*

The route to Stratford-upon-Avon now took them in a more easterly direction, and after about fifteen miles, as they approached Wootton Wawen near Henley-in-Arden, John Petre's attention was attracted by an old woman working in a field nearby.

'Master! Do you not see a troop of horse before you?' she cried as John and the others were about to pass her. Sure enough, about a mile down the road he saw a large detachment of Parliamentary troopers – possibly up to 500 men. They were dismounted, their horses put to grass while their riders relaxed by the side of the road. John was worried. They were unlikely to accost a lady like Jane Lane, and by that token her servant Will Jackson might be safe; but Petre himself had already been assaulted by troopers on two separate previous occasions on his travels and there was even the chance that their horses would be commandeered. He warned the group that it was too risky to proceed in this direction, but Charles didn't seem convinced and Petre noticed him saying something in a low voice to Jane Lane. She then suggested to her brother that they continue with caution and turn away if there was any sign of the troopers taking an interest in their arrival. But Colonel Lane sided with Petre and insisted upon them taking immediate avoiding action. At about this time, the Parliamentarians began to rise from their period of respite and prepare to mount up. Consequently, the little party veered away down a lane near the village of Bearley and followed a less direct route to their destination, taking them close to Snitterfield, after which they rejoined the main road they had previously been on. To reach their eventual goal of Long Marston they would need to cross the Avon near Stratford, but as they approached the river it turned out that their attempts to avoid the troopers had backfired. It transpired that this has also been their destination, and now some of them were loitering outside an inn on the road they were travelling along. However, to the relief of Petre and the others, the troops politely made way so they could pass through, and there was even a mutual doffing of hats and exchange of greetings. Here, Petre bade farewell to his travelling companions. He and Withy now took the road south-east towards their home at Horton in Buckinghamshire, leaving Lassels, Jane Lane and the man whom he thought of as Will Jackson, to press on for a further six miles roughly south-west to the place they were to stay for the night, the house of John Tombs in Long Marston.

Commentary:

- Poor Robert Swan the servant, was later, like many others, to petition the king for financial succour for his part in helping Charles. The petition stated that he 'has lived four years on his friends who cannot longer maintain him; has been three months in town relying on friends to make known his sad condition; has neither bread nor clothes, and being £200 in debt, dares not stir abroad for fear of being arrested'. Robert must have been overjoyed to learn that Charles remembered him, and how 'with how much fidelity he served him in his escape after the Battle of Worcester'. He was granted a pension of £60.
- Lassels' name is spelt thus pretty consistently in various contemporary accounts, but modern writers often refer to him as 'Lascelles'.
- The shop where the blacksmith Charles encountered is said to be attached to the Old Black Cross Inn, which still stands on Worcester Road, Bromsgrove and is reputed to be haunted – though not by Charles himself!
- The lane the party took near Snitterfield became known as King's Lane, which remains to this day.
- There seems to be no certainty as to whether the party crossed the Avon by bridge or ford. An ancestor of Tombs says it was Clopton Bridge – but one arch of that structure had already been destroyed in 1642 during the war.

Chapter 10

From Long Marston

We lay at a kinsman's, I think, of Mrs Lane's; neither the said kinsman, nor her a-fore-mentioned brother-in-law, knowing who I was. The next night we lay at Cirencester; and so from thence to Mr Norton's house, beyond Bristol...where, as soon as ever I came, Mrs Lane called the butler of the house… She bade him to take care of William Jackson, for that was my name, as having been lately sick of an ague, whereof she said I was still weak, and not quite recovered. And the truth is, my late fatigues and want of meat, had indeed made me look a little pale… Pope the butler took great care of me that night, I not eating, as I should have done, with the servants, upon account of my not being well.

The next morning I...went to the buttery hatch to get my breakfast; where I found Pope and two or three other men in the room... And as I was sitting there, there was one that looked like a country-fellow sat just by me, who...gave so particular an account of the battle of Worcester, to the rest of the company, that I concluded he must be one of Cromwell's soldiers. But I asking him, how 'he came to give so good an account of that battle?' He told me, he was in the King's regiment; by which I thought he meant one Colonel King's regiment. But questioning him further, I perceived that he had been in my regiment of guards... I asked him what a kind of man I was? To which he answered by describing exactly both my cloaths and my horse; and then looking upon me, he told me that the King was at least three fingers taller than I. Upon which I made what haste I could out of the buttery, for fear he should indeed know me, as being more afraid when I knew he was one of our own soldiers, than when I took him for one of the enemies.

So Pope and I went into the hall, and just as we came into it Mrs Norton was coming by thro' it; upon which, I plucking off my hat, and standing with my hat in my hand, as she past [sic] by, that Pope looked very earnestly in my face. But I took no notice of it, but put on my hat again, and went away, walking out of the house into the field. I had not been out half an hour, but coming back I went up to the chamber where I lay; and... Mr Lassells came to me, and in a little trouble said, what shall we do? I am afraid Pope knows you; for he says very positively to me that it is you, but I have denyed it. Upon which I...without more ado, asked him, whether he was a very honest man or no? Whereto he answering me, that he knew him to be so honest a fellow that he durst trust him with his life, as having been always on our side. I...thereupon sent for Pope, and told him, that I was very glad to meet him there, and would trust him with my life as an old acquaintance. Upon which, being a discreet fellow, he asked me what I intended to do? for, says he, I am extremely happy I know you, for otherways you might run great danger in this house. For though my master and mistress are good people, yet there are at this time one or two in it that are very great rogues; and I think I can be useful to you in any thing you will command me. Upon which I told him my design of getting a ship, if possible, at Bristol; and to that end bade him go that very day immediately to Bristol, to see if there were any ships going either to Spain or France, that I might get a passage away in.

So after Pope had been at Bristol to enquire for a ship, but could hear of none ready to depart...I betook myself to the advising afresh with my Lord Wilmot and Pope what was to be done. And the latter telling me that there lived somewhere in that country, upon the edge of Somersetshire, at Trent, within two miles of Sherburn, Frank Windham...who being my old acquaintance, and a very honest man, I resolved to go to his house. But the night before we were to go away...Mrs Norton, who was big with child, fell into labour, and miscarried of a dead child, and was very ill; so that we could not tell how in the world to find an excuse for Mrs Lane to leave her cousin in that condition; and indeed it was not safe to stay longer there, where there was so great resort of disaffected idle people.

At length, consulting with Mr Lassells, I thought the best way to counterfeit a letter from her father's house...to tell her that her father was extremely ill, and commanded her to come away immediately, for fear that she should not otherways find him alive; which letter Pope delivered so well, while they were all at supper, and Mrs Lane playing her part so dexterously, that all believed old Mr Lane to be indeed in great danger, and gave his daughter the excuse to go away with me the very next morning early.

King Charles, as dictated to Samuel Pepys

On Wednesday, 10 September, John Tombs' cook-maid at his house in Long Marston was asked by her master to prepare a meal for some visitors. His relatives, Colonel Lane, with his sister Jane and Henry Lassels, had arrived for an overnight stay. Seeing Mistress Lane's servant skulking in her kitchen, she decided to enlist his help. They had a new-fangled clockwork roasting jack hanging from one of the oak ceiling beams, and it would require winding up before the meat could be roasted. She asked the man to take care of this for her, but although he willingly set to his task, she could see that he was attempting to wind it the wrong way. She cried out a warning before he could damage the expensive machine.

'What countryman are you that know not how to wind up a jack?'

The servant sheepishly stopped trying to force the handle the wrong way and apologised. 'I am a poor tenant's son of Colonel Lane in Staffordshire. We seldom have roast meat; but when we have, we don't make use of a jack.'

This was enough to soothe the maid's annoyance and she allowed him to continue in the correct manner this time, while she got on with her own work.

John Tombs, 'but a little man, neat limbed, a little quick searching eie, sad, gray' was a Baptist divine and renowned preacher of about 50 years of age. His quick, searching eye didn't see through Charles' disguise during the course of his stay.

*

The next morning, Henry Lassels rose early and met up with Colonel Lane and Lord Wilmot, who had stayed the night at Packington Hall, the seat of Sir Clement Fisher. At this rendezvous, Wilmot proposed that Colonel Lane should make a trip to London to obtain travel documents allowing 'Will Jackson' to travel to France, and he duly left their little group to undertake this mission.

Lassels and the rest of the party took their leave of their host Mr Tombs, who was still unaware of the true identity of Will, the cack-handed kitchen servant.

They rode away from his fairly large, half-timbered but rather plain house, and trotted out of Long Marston (whose name well suited the straggling nature of the settlement – a long line of buildings beside the road heading south through the Cotswolds towards Chipping Campden). They passed through this town and then Stow-on-the-Wold, which must have awoken in Charles echoes of the defeat of one of his father's armies seven years previously. They had put between 35 and 40 miles behind them by the time they reached Cirencester, where they found rooms and a meal at the Crown Inn near the market place.

Lassels was to share a room with Charles, and as the 'gentleman' he was duly allocated the best bed, leaving Charles himself to make do with a truckle bed. However, as soon as the chamberlain had gone, Lassels insisted they swap and gave up best bed for the king.

On the Friday, they rejoined Jane Lane (Wilmot was still scouting around in the guise of a sporting gentleman out with his hawks) and were soon underway again. They pointed their horses in a south-westerly direction with what they hoped would be the final leg of the British leg of their trek: the port of Bristol and a ship to France.

*

Captain Matthew Huntley had been heavily engaged in the civil war, serving with the cavalry of Charles' cousin Prince Rupert in several major battles. He retreated to Boxwell Court, his country house near Leighterton, Gloucestershire, when the war was lost, but roused himself again to join Charles at Worcester. Possibly alerted in advance by the roaming Wilmot, he now received the little group of weary travellers at his home, a place where Rupert himself had stayed more than once. And this time there was no pretence. Charles was able to let down his guard and be himself in the presence of so loyal an officer. For safety's sake, though, Huntley led Charles out into a nearby wood while he rested and refreshed himself. As a reward, Charles gave the gallant Huntley one of his rings before he and his companions resumed their journey.

*

Jane Lane assumed her customary pillion position behind Charles as they moved on to Chipping Sodbury, which town they passed through without incident. Lassels rode close by, but Wilmot was still an outrider, having no contact with them during the actual journeying.

They entered Bristol some time after mid-day. It was a place unknown to Jane, but it was the city where Charles had been based for around five months during the civil war and he told her he wanted to make a slight detour. At the

62

age of fifteen, his father had made him the nominal captain-general of the Royalist forces in the west. Bristol eventually fell to Parliamentary forces (after Charles had already moved further west) and now he guided their horse so that he might cast a melancholy eye over the ruins of the castle, which Cromwell had ordered destroyed after the fall of the city.

They plodded on to Abbots Leigh in Somerset, about four miles east of Bristol, and by late afternoon reached the home of Jane's heavily pregnant close friend Ellen Norton. It was a grand Tudor mansion set in a sprawling estate and guarded by a tower-topped gatehouse. The house itself had three floors and twelve gables, with steps leading up to a central front entrance. It stood on the brow of a hill, from which Jane caught views of the Bristol Channel and the Welsh mountains as they approached.

It was a holiday, and house guests were gathered on a green at the front of the house playing bowls. As they drew nearer, Charles realised that he knew one of the spectators to the match – a physician called Thomas Gorges who had been a court chaplain during his father's reign. Jane therefore saw to it that Charles avoided the group by taking their horse directly to the stables, while she would report directly to Ellen and establish his cover story. She was led up to the chamber where her cousin lay in confinement, her swollen belly attesting to advanced stage of her pregnancy.

After they had exchanged greetings, Jane mentioned her concerns over her travelling companion, a 'good youth' called William Jackson whose father had allowed him to escort her on the long journey – but who had been suffering from an ague. He certainly wasn't fit to help with work below stairs, and in fact she hoped a good room could be arranged for him in which to recuperate. The fact that Charles was weary from continued travelling and the stress of knowing he might be caught at any moment with an inevitable execution to follow, together with a rather meagre and irregular diet, meant that his drawn and pallid complexion would help to substantiate this cover story. As a result, a boy was dispatched to the stables to call William and show him to the room that had been allocated to him. Jane then spoke to the Nortons' butler, a man called John Pope, and asked him to take special care of her man William Jackson, explaining about his illness. This sensible and well-meant gesture was to complicate matters somewhat before too long.

*

John Pope, the butler, waited at table during supper that night. This was something of a career change for him. He had served in the Royalist army under Colonel Bagot at the taking of Lichfield during the civil war; before that, he had been a falconer at the court of Charles I. He had reported to Sir Thomas Jermyn, the Groom of the Bedchamber to the young Prince Charles, when he was staying at Richmond.

A broth was served and Jane Lane took up a small dish and filled it with the steaming liquid. She summoned Pope and asked him to take it to William Jackson's room along with some bread and to see whether he felt well enough to manage it. The room that Pope entered was small, but perfectly warm thanks to a blazing fire; tapestries hung on the walls depicting African scenes of exotic animals and mothers carrying babies in slings on their backs. There was also a striking wax bust of the mistress of the house on display in the invalid's room. But these weren't the things that captured Pope's attention the most – for, though it barely seemed possible, he believed he recognized this young man...

*

Thomas Gorges was a Somerset man from a good family, but he too had found himself on a different career trajectory in recent years. He had been a priest, but under the current puritanical regime it wasn't healthy to be identified as such and he had turned towards medicine. He had thus taken a 'professional' interest in Mistress Lane's ailing groom whose health she seemed so concerned about, and plied her with questions about him. How long had it been since his ague had left him? Had he been purged? The lady fielded all his questions, yet he still felt he might be of service in the matter and when supper was over, he took himself off to William Jackson's room.

When he entered, the groom appeared to be shuffling across the bed, away from the light of the candle beside it, and casting himself in shadow. Gorges took the young man's pulse and tried to engage him in conversation, but William, though remaining polite, answered only perfunctorily and soon told Gorges that if he didn't mind, he would like to try to get some sleep. Gorges took the hint and went back to see Jane, telling her that he believed William would recover well enough, but to be on the safe side gave her advice on what to do if he were to suffer a relapse. He left Leigh Court the next morning.

*

One of the guests at Leigh Court had a story to tell, for he had a great deal of knowledge pertaining to the recent Battle of Worcester. He was regaling the company, one of whom was Pope the butler, in the buttery at breakfast when the tall groom arrived who had been keeping himself to himself since arrival. The rumour was that he was recovering from illness – but when they took their seats the groom sat beside the man and took an immediate interest in the tale of the fight as he ate his bread and butter and drank his ale.

How was it, Will Jackson wondered, that he knew so much about what happened at Worcester? The guest explained that he had, in fact, fought in the battle itself, in Major Broughton's regiment (the major himself had been captured and imprisoned).

William casually asked what the king was like. 'Have you ever seen him?' 'Twenty times!'

The man proceeded to describe the Charles' appearance in perfect and accurate detail – then studied Will Jackson closely for a moment before declaring that His Majesty was appreciably taller. Jane Lane's groom thanked the man, then quickly made his excuses and left the buttery.

*

Pope left the buttery with William Jackson and in the hall, they encountered Ellen Norton. Charles respectfully removed his hat until the mistress of the house had passed by and Pope took the opportunity of studying his face again. Now, he had no doubt in his mind as to who 'William Jackson' really was. As soon as the young man had gone upstairs to his room, John Pope went to see Jane Lane's cousin and travelling companion, Henry Lassels, and told him that he was certain as to the identity of their travelling companion. Lassels flatly denied it, and there was little else Pope could say – for the time being.

*

Lassels made straight for Charles' cosy little room.

'What shall we do? I am afraid Pope knows you, for he says very positively to me that it is you, but I have denied it.'

The king was disappointed, but when he had thought about it for a moment, he asked Lassels whether he considered Pope to be totally trustworthy. Lassels had no hesitation in describing Pope as a committed and loyal Royalist, one whom he would trust his with his own life (which in telling Pope the truth he would, in effect, be doing). On balance, Charles decided that it would be better to take him into their confidence than leaving him snooping and harbouring his suspicions. He asked that Pope be brought to him.

*

Pope answered the summons immediately, and the young king told him how very glad he was that their paths had crossed here, and how he would trust him with his life as an old acquaintance.

'What do you intend to do?' Pope asked. 'I am extremely happy I know you, for otherways you might run great danger in this house.' He went on to explain that although he could vouch for the Nortons, whose house it was, there were others present about whom he had his suspicions. Pope offered to help in any way he could.

Charles told Pope there was something he might help with in his plan to find a vessel at Bristol and asked him go there without delay to see if there were any ships lying there bound Spain or France onto which he might be smuggled. During the conversation, Charles also let Pope know that Lord Wilmot was due to meet him here this very day. Pope was pleased that his king had confided in him about this, because there were several currently at Leigh Court who were bound to recognize him. Because of this, he volunteered to intercept Wilmot on his way to the house. This he did, meeting Wilmot a mile or two from Leigh Court and seeing to it that he held off till it was dark, then led him to a back door of Norton's mansion and straight to Charles' chamber.

*

Pope now undertook his other important task and took himself off to the harbour at Bristol for news of ships preparing to leave for the Continent. Frustratingly, there were no vessels scheduled to leave for several weeks, which was far too long for Charles to risk waiting. He did, however, conjure up an alternative plan when he returned to Abbots Leigh and met Charles and Wilmot again. There was someone known to himself and the king who lived in Somerset called Frank Wyndham. He was the brother of Sir Edmund Wyndham, the Knight Marshal (responsible for keeping order in the King's Court) and lived at a place called Trent, near Sherborne. It was quite a distance – over forty miles south of Abbots Leigh – but Wyndham had fought on the king's side in the war, and Charles confirmed that he was 'old acquaintance, and a very honest man'. (Christabella, the wife of his eldest brother had been Charles' nurse when he was a baby). After conferring with Jane Lane and Lassels, it was decided that Trent was to be the next destination on this seemingly never-ending flight to freedom.

*

Wilmot arrived at Leigh on Saturday, 13 September, having spent the night in Gloucestershire. While on his roving commission, he had come across Captain Thomas Abington, one of his officers during the civil war, who had taken him to the home of a friend. Not long after his arrival, Jane Lane came to him and told him about Charles' plan to move on to Colonel Wyndham's house at Trent. Once he had been satisfied that this was a safe and expedient plan, he conferred with Charles, who asked him to go on ahead to alert Wyndham to their imminent arrival. He set out again the same day, with his hawk as before. This time he was guided by Henry Rogers, a servant who had showed him the way to Leigh, and Robert Swan, who had accompanied him to Leigh Court.

*

Sometime during the night of Sunday, 14 September, Jane Lane was woken by a commotion at Leigh Court. Her close friend Ellen Norton had gone into labour. As the night progressed, the reports from the labour room indicated that things weren't going well and eventually news was brought that she had given birth to a still-born child and was herself seriously ill. Much as Jane was concerned for Ellen's welfare, she could not ignore the fact that the following day had been earmarked for her departure with Charles and the journey to Trent. Jane conferred with Charles and Lassels. Despite their fears for Mrs Norton, it was too dangerous for Charles to remain in one place for so long – his stay at Abbots Leigh had already been longer than any other on the journey so far and this in a place where numerous people were being entertained, some of whose loyalty couldn't be counted on. But what reason for their departure could be given that wouldn't make Jane look callous, and perhaps even arouse suspicion?

It was Charles who came up with the idea. They would concoct a letter from Jane's family informing her that her father was dangerously ill himself. If she didn't set off to see him straight away, she might not see him alive again.

Jane was at supper that evening when the dependable Pope arrived and solemnly delivered the message. Along with Pope, Jane acted her part so believably as to arouse concern and sympathy from all those present and paved the way for a hasty departure from Leigh Court.

The following morning, Tuesday, 16 September, Jane mounted up behind Charles and they rode away from Abbots Leigh after a four day stay: heading north initially to fit in with their cover story of Jane's return home to be with her ailing father; but as soon as they dared they turned south, following a route deeper into the West Country and, hopefully, a port where a ship might be found.

Commentary:

- John Tombs (also 'Toombs', 'Tombes' and 'Tomes') was hauled before the local magistrate after the king's visit, causing him soon to after flee the county to France. He lost part of his estate, but as happened with several others, amends were made after the Restoration. His house (known now as King's Lodge) still stands, including, according to an estate agent's details issued when it was up for sale in 2018 (for £1.3 million!) the fire over which Charles operated the spit. The roasting jack itself was at one time exhibited in London. It was returned to the Tombs house and was still there, displayed in glass by the fire as late as 1913 when it was mentioned in *Summer Days in Shakespeare Land* by Charles G Harper. By this time, the house had been much altered and the kitchen now formed part of the living area. At some point the jack must have been taken away, because unfortunately it is no longer a fixture.

- A pub in Leighterton near Boxwell Court called the Royal Oak, is said to be so named to commemorate Charles' stay, and part of a wood at Boxwell acquired the name King's Walk. Boxwell Court was searched by Cromwellian troopers after the battle of Worcester, and Captain Matthew Huntley (whose uncle John had fought against Charles' father in the civil war) was concealed by his daughter Lady Winyard. There is a family tradition that Huntley, who may well have known Charles, escorted him to Bristol. The fact that his name does not crop up in any of the various accounts makes it unlikely, and the story of Matthew showing Charles to the woods, and for all we know even the first part of the way after leaving Boxwell, has perhaps grown in the telling.

- When I was looking into George Norton (see below) I spotted something about the relationship between his wife and Jane Lane. Allan Fea, who is considered an authority, categorically states that the references to her being related to Ellen are wrong – they were just close friends.

- Shortly after the Restoration, George Norton was knighted for his services to the king at this time. Thankfully, his wife Ellen did survive the traumatic delivery of her dead child.

- The same Lady Wood who left the account of hearing Charles tell his mother about Careless shaking and quaking in the oak tree, also recorded being told that: 'Charles feigning sickness most of the time and sitting in the chimney corner, Mrs Lane would say "This boy will never recover – he'll ne're be good again…".'. This also doesn't ring quite true. For one thing Charles spent most of his time in his room to avoid the numerous guests who were being entertained at that time. Jane Lane appears to have spread the story that Charles was in fact recuperating from an ague which had passed rather than being in the throes of one, which also doesn't fit in with such pessimism regarding his health.

- The Lane family claimed to be the only ones granted the right to three royal lions in their coat of arms as a result of the part Jane and her cousin played in helping the king.

Chapter 11

Trent

Accordingly the next morning we went directly to Trent to
Frank Windham's house and lay that night at Castle-Cary...
and the next night came to Trent, where I had appointed my
Lord Wilmot to meet me... When we came to Trent, my Lord
Wilmot and I advised with Frank Windham, whether he had
any acquaintance at any sea-town upon the coast of Dorset
or Devonshire; who told me that he was very well acquainted
with Gyles Strangways, and that he would go directly to
him, and inform himself whether he might not have some
acquaintance at Weymouth or Lyme, or some of those parts.
But Gyles Strangways proved not to have any... He desired
Frank Windham to try what he could do...it being unsafe for
him to be found busy upon the sea coast. But withal he sent me
three hundred broad pieces, which he knew were necessary for
me in the condition I was now in; for I durst carry no money
about me in those mean cloaths, and my hair cut short, but
about ten or twelve shillings in silver.

Frank Windham...went himself to Lyme, and spoke with
a merchant there, to hire a ship for my transportation, being
forced to acquaint him that it was I that was to be carried out.
The merchant [Ellesdon] undertook it...and accordingly hired
a vessel for France, appointing a day for my coming to Lyme
to embark.

King Charles, as dictated to Samuel Pepys

Edward Kirton was waiting at a designated spot on the road between
Bristol and Castle Cary. He was in his mid-sixties, a local man who had
served as a Member of Parliament before the civil war. There had been
times when he had alienated himself from Charles I, but he was a recusant

(someone – usually Catholic – who refused to attend Anglican services) and when war came was fined for supporting the Royalist cause. He had been briefed by Lord Wilmot, who had ridden ahead of Charles, Jane Lane and Lassels. Towards mid-day, Kirton saw three people approaching on horseback. One of the horses was double-mounted, bearing a young man and woman – and Kirton soon realised that the man was King Charles.

Once Kirton had revealed his identity to them, it was decided that since there were Parliamentary troopers in the area and Kirton was steward to the Marquis of Hertford and a known Royalist, Castle Cary itself was too risky and a safer place was needed where Charles could spend the night. Thus they turned off the road to Castle Cary for just a short distance and went to the home of the Collins family in Lower Ansford. However, not long after their arrival word came to Kirton that Parliamentary searchers were coming their way. He hurried Charles and Jane Lane to a gully on the edge of the village, where they laid low.

*

Late on the same day, Frank Wyndham received an unexpected visitor at his home in the picturesque village of Trent, not far from Sherborne to the south-east and Yeovil to the south-west, and about twelve miles south of Castle Cary. It was a man called Rogers, informing him that a certain gentleman, a friend of his, was waiting nearby and wished to speak to him on an important matter. Puzzled, Wyndham asked the man who his caller was and what he wanted, but Rogers could only reply that he knew nothing about it, and only knew his travelling companion as 'Mr Morton'. Wyndham went outside and found his visitor hovering by the stables; he bore a hawk on his fist. Although it was still not quite light, Wyndham immediately recognized him, greeting him warmly as 'My lord Wilmot'. Wilmot was a little put out that he had been recognized so easily, but Wyndham told him it was hardly surprising, considering that not only had they served together in the army, but Wilmot had made no attempt at disguising himself apart from his hawk and lure. But when Wyndham enquired after the purpose of his former commanding officer's visit, it was his turn to be surprised.

The shocking but joyful news was that Charles, the rightful king of England, had not been killed at or after Worcester as had been widely reported, but was safe and well and endeavouring to make his way to a port and hopefully the Continent. Wyndham assured Wilmot that 'for His Majesty's preservation I would value neither my life, family

nor fortune, and would never injure His Majesty's confidence of me.'
He took Wilmot indoors, where they settled down and listened as the
earl told him of all that had happened up to this point in the odyssey.
Wilmot stayed the night, and in the morning, Wyndham drew his wife
and mother into the plot.

Their main concern was how to smuggle Charles in and hide him when
they had so much company at Trent just then – over twenty guests. It was
decided that a select few could and should be trusted with the truth and
these included Juliana Coningsby (Lady Wyndham's niece) and Henry
Peters, Frank Wyndham's servant whose Royalist convictions were not in
doubt. Next, they considered which chambers were fittest for His Majesty's
reception, and it was agreed that Anne Wyndham's suite of four rooms
would fit the bill. They also cooked up reasons to get as many people as
possible out of the way at the time Charles was due to arrive. The planning
taken care of, they could only wait for the king's arrival and hope, with so
many servants and visitors populating the house, that nothing went wrong
that might jeopardise his safety.

*

Not long after her guests had left, Mrs Collins was piously reading her Bible
when the search party came knocking at her door. She was soon able to
satisfy the Parliamentarians that she wasn't harbouring the king or any other
Worcester fugitives, and the hunters took themselves off to the local rectory.

*

Once the coast was clear, Kirton guided Charles to his brother's house in
Lower Ansford, where his important and much sought-after guest was able
to spend the night of 16 September unhindered.

*

It was mid-morning on Wednesday, 17 September, and two people were out
walking in the meadows in vicinity of Trent House, an old manor house right
beside the parish church. One was 41-year-old Colonel Frank Wyndham,
who had stoutly defended Dunster Castle, some fifty miles to the west
(where Charles II had stayed just months earlier) during a prolonged siege
by Parliamentary forces for as long as humanly possible, before finally
surrendering with honour intact. With him was his 19-year-old wife Anne,
and they were out on the pretext of going for a stroll – but in reality, they
were anxiously awaiting an important arrival.

At around ten o'clock two horses came into view: one carrying a lone rider, and the other bearing a gentlewoman behind a man in groom's clothing. In case Wyndham was in any doubt as to their identity, he soon heard a voice cry,

'Frank, Frank, how dost thou do?' It was His Majesty King Charles the Second.

It was a momentous moment and Wyndham was pleased to find the young king in such good spirits. But after a hasty greeting, Wyndham was keen to get his visitors safely indoors and away from prying eyes. Charles was surreptitiously led to a back entrance, while Wyndham openly escorted Jane and Lassels and announced them as relatives, just here for an overnight stay.

Wyndham then smuggled the king, along with his two other guests, directly to Anne's own room as planned, with its dark oak panels and beams. Some of those panels served a secret purpose and would prove useful in due course. Jane Lane was only to stay the night and then return home. In the meantime, it was decided that when anyone was within earshot she would be referred to as 'Cousin' and treated like an old friend. Now, Jane and Anne Wyndham went downstairs, and Lord Wilmot was shown in to confer with Charles and Frank Wyndham and plan their next move. Wyndham offered to visit a trusted friend and cousin who lived at Melbury Sampford, about ten miles to the south near Dorchester, in the hope that he might be able to suggest a vessel or an owner of one.

*

One of Wyndham's maids received a summons from his 'cousin'. Going up to his room, the tall groom who had accompanied her asked her if she knew why the bells in the church, adjacent to the house, were being rung. She told him what she had heard herself – Parliamentary soldiers returning from the Battle of Worcester had appeared in the village making a big fuss about their victory and the 'death' of the king: guns were being fired, bonfires lit, and toasts drunk. One soldier in particular was boasting that the fine buff coat he was wearing was from the corpse of the great man himself. This district, she explained to Charles, was generally for Parliament – hence the ringing of the bells and making of bonfires. His only comment before she returned to her duties was 'Alas, poor people...'

*

Colonel Giles Strangways was another who had fought for the Royalists during the civil war. He was a ruddy faced, blunt-spoken man in his mid-thirties, who had for a time been a prisoner in the Tower of London. On the morning of 18 September, he received a visit from his acquaintance Frank Wyndham, who enigmatically suggested that they took a walk in the parkland surrounding his house. Only once they were away from curious eyes and ears did Wyndham explain the true reason for his visit. Unfortunately, Strangways knew of no vessel that would serve the purpose Wyndham had revealed; there were several at Weymouth who might have been able to help, but because of their support for the Royalist cause they had either been exiled or had fled abroad for their own safety. Neither had he contacts in other ports, such as Lyme and Poole. The only assistance he could extend to his king was financial. He gave Wyndham 300 gold sovereigns, worth around £100, and suggested he try his luck in the busy little fishing port of Lyme Regis.

*

Early on the same morning, Jane Lane, accompanied by Cornet Henry Lassels, also rode away from Trent Court. Having courageously accomplished the vital but perilous duty that fate had placed before them, entailing a trek of at least 167 miles, (but probably more) Jane took her leave of her grateful royal travelling companion for the last time, and began the long journey back to Bentley in Warwickshire.

*

Captain William Ellesdon, from a family of staunch Royalists, was the second friend of Frank Wyndham to receive a visit from him that day. He was a captain in the army rather than the navy, but he already had experience in such nautical exploits, having previously helped Sir John Berkeley to flee to the continent. When Wyndham arrived at his house near Lyme and explained the purpose of his mission, Ellesdon, who had recently married a wealthy Presbyterian, was delighted to be able to help. He immediately sent a servant down to the Custom House in Lyme to see if they had a record of anyone scheduled to sail to France in the near future, and his man soon returned with the name of a likely candidate who lived in nearby Charmouth. It seemed that luck was on their side, because not only was this mariner known to Ellesdon – he was a tenant of his – but Ellesdon knew him to be a supporter of the king.

They immediately went to their horses and set off to interview him but took a slight detour along the way because Ellesdon had a departure point in mind, should this seafarer agree to their plan. It was a place away from the road, houses and Lyme's busy harbour, and Wyndham agreed that it would suit their needs perfectly.

*

Stephen Limbry, the master of a small coasting vessel of thirty tons based at Lyme, was at home in Charmouth when he received a message begging him to meet his landlord Captain Ellesdon at the Queen's Arms. He hastened to the inn and found that Ellesdon had another man with him who was introduced as 'Captain Norris'. These two had a proposition to put to him. They knew he was planning to sail to France and hoped that he might be able to add a friend who had had a 'finger in the pie' at Worcester to his cargo.

As soon as Worcester was mentioned, Limbry was worried. This sounded like no small matter and could land him in big trouble should they be found out – even putting his life in danger. But his visitors both pressured and reassured him and added that he would be paid £60 for his troubles, half in advance and half on his return from France bearing a note from the people he had transported confirming that they had been safely delivered. Limbry was still hesitant. Although he was scheduled to sail to St Malo in due course, he had only recently returned from a French trip and it might look suspicious if he set off again too soon. He would certainly require a further nine shillings to cover the ballasting of his ship, which Ellesdon, having already made a generous offer, refused to pay. On being assured of the absolute secrecy of the mission, Limbry finally agreed to transport the mystery Royalists. Ellesdon and 'Norris' told him of their preferred rendezvous place, and it was arranged that his small ship would be sailed close to the shore on the night of 22 September and allowed to be beached as the tide went out, where the passengers could come aboard, then set sail in the morning when the incoming tide refloated the vessel.

*

Harry Peters, Frank Wyndham's servant, made his way to Charmouth on a mission allotted to him by his master on his arrival back at Trent. There was to be a fair in Lyme on the scheduled day of departure, so accommodation in town would probably get booked up quickly. Peters, therefore, made his way to the Queen's Arms, where, with something of a nod and a wink over a glass of wine with Margaret Wade, the proprietress, Peters explained that he was after a couple of rooms but that it was important discretion be guaranteed – for a young man and his sweetheart were involved in a plan of elopement, and for that reason they would probably slip away some time during the night after taking rest and refreshments. Mrs Wade was understanding and Peters left the Queen's Arms having reserved the best two rooms for the night of the 22 September at a cost of five shillings.

*

The 'elopement' drama dreamt up by Wyndham and Ellesdon featured not Charles but Wilmot in the male lead, but they still needed a person to play the part of his lordship's beloved – which is how Julia Coninsgby, Anne Wyndham's niece and live-in companion at Trent Court, found herself stepping into Jane Lane's shoes. Just as with Jane, she shared the same horse as Charles when they sallied forth, with Julia riding behind Charles, Colonel Wyndham showing the way and Lord Wilmot and Henry Peters hanging back as if not part of the group. It was nearly thirty miles to Charmouth, but along the way there were to be a couple of stops. First, Wyndham led Julia and Charles to Clapton Court near Crewkerne.

*

The tenant to whom Captain Ellesdon's brother let out his secluded house at Monkton Wyld, near Bridport, answered a knock at the door and was greeted by Ellesdon himself. His house was close to the London road, and the former Royalist soldier informed the tenant that he had arranged to meet some friends here at about the time when the coach to London was due to pass by. Not long afterwards, a small group of travellers arrived, including a young man and woman sharing a horse and they withdrew for a private conversation.

*

Everything was arranged. Ellesdon informed Charles that Limbry's ship was ready to sail at the appointed hour, and the hostess of the Queen's Arms had accepted the elopement cover story and so was unlikely to ask too many questions. Limbry, the ship's captain, had told his sailors a quite different tale to the 'young lovers' one given to the landlady of the Queen's Arms. This new artifice was that Wilmot was a merchant by the name of Payne, slipping away in the dead of night for fear of arrest after some disastrous business matter. He had goods being held by an agent in St Malo and needed to quietly slip out of England to get them before his creditors tracked him down. He would be taking with him his servant – a role Charles was by now used to playing. Ellesdon encouraged Wilmot and Charles to ad lib on this unfortunate turn of events on 'Payne's' affair once they were on board in order to reinforce the story.

At what they believed to be their final parting, Charles dipped his hand into his pocket and held something out to Ellesdon, saying apologetically that he had nothing of greater value to give him for his help. The item the merchant took from him was a gold coin. It had had a hole bored through the middle, presumably by Charles during an idle hour. It was to remain in his family for many generations.

Commentary:

- I have followed the version of the Castle Cary episode showing Charles avoiding Castle Cary Manor and going to Lower Ansford, which Allan Fea in *The Flight of the King* says is backed up by local tradition, but other accounts do have him sleeping the night in Castle Cary itself.
- Giles Strangways was on the list of proposed Knights of the Royal Oak (see Chapter 21).
- Edward Kirton died less than three years after playing his part in Charles' escape.
- Jane Lane is often referred to as 'Mrs Lane' in the contemporary accounts, but she was then unmarried. She became Lady Fisher upon marrying the Sir Clement at whose house Wilmot and Colonel Lane stayed. Before that, in October 1651, Jane and her brother discovered that someone close to them had betrayed their secret. They made their way to Yarmouth in disguise, and managed to get a boat to France, and Jane was given a position with the Princess of Orange. The following month Jane Lane, accompanied by brother John, visited Charles in Paris, where they were warmly welcomed. Charles gave her a sort of royal reception, accompanied by the Dukes of York and Gloucester. Upon setting eyes on Jane again for the first time since they had shared their dangerous adventure, he took her hand, crying, 'Welcome, my life!'. Jane and Charles subsequently kept up a correspondence with each other, and he signed his letters 'Your most assured and constant friend, Charles R'.
- Colonel Lane returned to England in the spring of 1652 and was arrested for his loyalty to king. A few months later, Charles

wrote to Jane regretting he couldn't afford to reward her at that time. This was excusable – he was never well off in exile – but he didn't forget his debt to her. There have been rumours down the years that Jane and Charles were involved in some sort of relationship during the course of their adventure. They were two young, single people thrown together during a period of shared heightened emotions, so it would hardly be surprising; but there is no evidence, and anyway it's hard to see how they would have found the time and privacy to have conducted a secret liaison considering their circumstances. But it's interesting to note that Jane was by far the best rewarded of all those who helped the king. After the Restoration, she was granted £1,000 (more than double the amount almost anyone else received) in addition to which she was given the gift of an extremely expensive jewel, a gold watch, a snuff box containing Charles' portrait, and other presents. Colonel John Lane was offered a peerage but reluctantly turned it down, 'not having the means to support his dignity'.

- The house owned by the Ellesdons where Charles stopped on his way to Charmouth still exists, on a little lane dipping sharply down off the former Roman road which is now the A35. Its modern name has echoes of its history – 'Elsdon's Farm' (on Elsdon's Lane) and it bears a plaque commemorating the royal visit. A contemporary local claimed that the tenant did know that one of his guests was Charles and came to him for advice on whether to help him. The neighbour's opinion was that since the king 'was come for safety under his roof, he should in nowise betray him but lett him goe as hee came... .'

- A cap and vest said to have been made for Charles during his time at Trent were preserved and remained in the family for some centuries, as were forks and spoons he used while there.

- At the Restoration, Frank Wyndham was made a baronet and he and his wife were paid a lump sum and granted pensions, as were the two maids who waited on Charles.

Chapter 12

Charmouth

And accordingly we set out from Frank Windham's, and to cover the matter the better, I rode before a cousin of Frank Windham's, one Mrs Judith [Juliana] Coningsby, still going by the name of William Jackson…. I stayed some four or five days at Frank Windham's house, and was known to most of his family. This merchant having appointed us to come to Lyme, we…were directed from him to a little village [Charmouth] hard by Lyme the vessel being to come out of the cobb at Lyme, and come to a little creek that was just by this village, whither we went, and to send their boat ashore to take us in at the said creek, and carry us over to France, the wind being then very good at north.

So we sat up that night, expecting the ship to come out, but she failed us… At last, we resolved to go to a place called Burport, [Bridport] about four miles from Lyme, and there stay till my Lord Wilmot should bring us news, whether the vessel could be had the next night or no, and the reason of her last nights failure.

King Charles, as dictated to Samuel Pepys

Juliana Coningsby peered over Charles' shoulder at the fleeting glimpses of countryside visible through the trees as they followed narrow the road gradually descending towards the sea. Eventually, she saw view of cliffs towards Bridport in the distance, and not long afterwards they arrived at the Queen's Arms in Charmouth. Once Wilmot had joined them to play the other half of the eloping couple, they ventured into the inn. Ellesdon went off to see Limbry to let them know that all had so far gone according to plan and to pave the way for the next stage of the venture, while Wyndham and his servant Peters went to the embarkation spot on the coast to await the boat. The end of Charles' mission was in sight.

*

Margaret Wade at the Queen's Arms was a busy woman. It was one of nearby Lyme's regular fairs today; the inn was bustling and it was a good job that the secret lovers had booked their room in advance or they might have had to look elsewhere. When they arrived as arranged, she greeted the couple and their travelling companion and showed them to their rooms.

*

It was growing dark. Wyndham and Peters began to feel the early chill of autumn as they lurked by the beach, waiting for a sign of Limbry's boat. Had their plan been undone? Had Limbry been arrested? They waited and waited.

*

The ostler of the Queen's Arms had grown suspicious. Mrs Wade had told him about her mystery guests – and he just happened to be a soldier under Captain Macy, commanding a company of foot based at Lyme. The ostler began to wonder whether there wasn't something about them that made them different from the run-of-the-mill guest and usual fair-goers that went beyond the story she had been told. Because of this, he had been keeping a wary eye on these visitors. He had noticed the mysterious nocturnal comings and goings of some of the party and the way the others remained cloistered away, not joining in with the general company in the downstairs rooms. Despite Mrs Wade's acceptance of the purported reason for all this, he suspected there might be another explanation. In fact, he thought he knew what it was...

*

Mrs Limbry had had a good outing to Lyme fair. She was welcomed by her two daughters and her seafaring husband upon her return – but it wasn't long before events unfolded which were to well and truly ruin her day. It started when Stephen called for his sea chest. Sea chest? He had only recently come home and as far as she was aware, he had no goods that needed transporting overseas. When she asked him what was going on, Stephen revealed that his cargo was a human one – and that he was being paid much more to transport it than he would for any of his usual merchandise.

Mrs Limbry was a shrewd woman, and while she had been at the fair, she had noticed the posters offering a reward of £1,000 for the capture of Charles Stuart in his flight from Worcester. More worryingly, she had also read of the dark warnings regarding what would happen to those caught helping him avoid arrest. She put two and two together and when her husband went into their bedroom to collect some clothing for the voyage, she deftly locked him in. A violent argument ensued, but Mrs Limbry stood firm. She wasn't going to allow the actions of her husband to bring the whole family to ruin, and even threatened to report Stephen to Captain Macy and his soldiers stationed in town if he should attempt to escape and fulfil his mission. Limbry's barque stayed moored in the Cobb.

*

As the clock continued to tick, Wilmot, waiting with the king, stayed by the window of their room waiting for them to be summoned. Whenever he saw the light of a lantern outside the inn he hurried out, hoping the call had finally come. But it proved to be a false alarm every time.

*

Wyndham could wait no longer. The appointed hour had gone and he could see in the moonlight that the tide that would have brought Limbry's ship in close to shore had now turned. Whatever the reason might be for the vessel's non-appearance – and the implications were worrying – it was now impossible for the plan to be effected tonight. Wyndham told his man Harry Peters that they were leaving and they began to trudge back to the Queen's Arms.

They hadn't walked far when he tensed – a little group of figures emerged out of the gloom, heading his way. In the midnight darkness of the secluded footpath, he thought, as they came closer, that the leading figure resembled Stephen Limbry, but trailing after him were a woman and two girls so it didn't make sense. It was too risky to stop them and engage them in conversation to make sure and he carried on past. Wyndham sent word to the king surmising that Limbry had been unable to man his ship because, with it being the fair, his sailors couldn't be induced to leave the local ale houses and go aboard. He added that he believed it to be too risky for Charles to prolong his stay in Charmouth.

*

When Limbry and his family arrived at the designated landing place on the coast to break the bad news that the voyage was cancelled, it was deserted. They were too late, and there was nothing left for it but for Limbry but to turn on his heels and head disconsolately back to his house.

*

The Queen's Arms' stableman slipped out of the inn the following morning, Tuesday, 23 September. He decided that the first person he ought to put his suspicions to was Westley, the local parson. But when he arrived at the priest's house, he was informed by the servant that the master was at prayer with his family and couldn't be disturbed. The ostler wended his way back to the inn – but he wasn't going to let it drop as easily as that.

*

Their plan in tatters, Wilmot conferred with Charles, Wyndham and Julia Coninsgby, and it was decided to heed Wyndham's advice and quickly move on. The king and Julia would make the short trip eastwards along the coast, in the opposite direction to Lyme, and head for Bridport. Lord Wilmot and Harry Peters wanted to see if they could find out more about what had – or had not – happened from Ellesdon, so would delay their departure by a few hours. Wilmot's horse in any case, needed a new shoe. He arranged for the ostler to take it to Hammet, a local blacksmith.

*

Hammet, the Charmouth blacksmith, was for Parliament. He knew his job, and he knew his horse shoes. So it was that when his equally republican friend the stableman of the Queen's Arms brought in a horse that had lost a shoe, it didn't escape his attention that this animal had made a long journey, and was shod with the distinctive ironwork of more than one county; none of them local – and one of them Worcestershire. He mentioned this to Margaret Wade's man, who revealed to him his earlier suspicions. The ostler scurried back to Westley and this time was able to spill out his tale to him. They both quickly made their way to the Queen's Arms.

*

Margaret Wade's ostler arrived at the inn in company with Westley the parson, asking after their recent shady visitors – only to find that they had already departed.

'Why, how now, Margaret. You are a maid of honour now?' declared Westley.

'What mean you by that?'

'Why, Charles Stuart lay at your house last night and kissed you at his departure – so that now you can't but be a maid of honour.'

Mrs Wade didn't take too kindly to this and called him a 'scurvy-conditioned man' for trying to spread stories that might get her into trouble. 'But if I thought it was the king, as you say it was, I would think the better of my lips all my life. And so, Mr Parson, get out of my house or I'll get those who shall kick you out.'

Westley angrily turned on his heels and left – but he still wasn't finished.

*

Mr Butler was a local justice of the peace. It was in this capacity that he received a deputation from Charmouth consisting of the Ostler, Parson Westley and Hammet the blacksmith, with a strange tale to tell about a visit by Charles Stuart himself, last heard of at Worcester. The two men were adamant that he had stayed the night at Mrs Wade's inn – but when pressed, the only evidence they had was some unexplained night time activity by one of the group of travellers and a well-travelled horse with a shoe that may have originated in Worcester. There had been many alarms raised around the country over supposed sightings of the young king, but Mr Butler wasn't about to become embroiled in such a wild goose chase and dismissed his petitioners forthwith. The disillusioned Hammet had done his bit and dropped the matter. If Butler wanted to miss the opportunity of fame and fortune, that was his lookout. But the obdurate stableman wasn't ready to let the matter lie just yet.

*

There were plenty of travellers on the road to Bridport, and one of them had been a servant to Charles I and knew the royal family well. It therefore came as a great shock to him to recognize that one of the parties he encountered on his way had among them his former master's son, the heir to the throne. A little older than he remembered him for sure, but it was certainly Charles. But this former servant was both loyal and a quick thinker. Seeing the king dressed as a commoner and sharing a horse with a lady as if acting as her servant, the man made eye contact with Charles but exchanged greetings with them in the same casually affable way that he had with everyone else he had met on the road – but he knew that Charles knew. The two men continued on their way without a glance back.

*

Margaret Wade's ostler's next port of call was his old captain, Macy whom he met at around mid-day. Macy was much easier to persuade than Butler had been, and immediately visited the inn to try to ascertain when the guests in question had left and what direction they had been heading in. It wasn't long before he had mounted his horse and was making all haste towards Bridport at the head of a group of soldiers.

Commentary:

- Limbry was later to claim that the sole reason for his not weighing anchor and transporting Charles as arranged was that Ellesdon never gave him the promised advance, and that 'whatever hath been set to the contrary was notoriously false'. However, the generally accepted story (also said to have been 'given under his own hand') is the version related above – that he was locked in his own house by his wife. The only suspicion left hanging over this 'true' account is that it seems to have been supplied by Ellesdon, who of course would have had good reason to exonerate himself – especially if he kept any of the money intended to pay Limbry.
- Twenty years later, Charles made a nostalgic return to some of the places on and around the south coast where he had spent his last few days before going into exile. In the summer of 1671 he rode from Lyme to Charmouth, where guns were fired and food and drink were laid on. In Axminster the church bells were rung as Charles passed through.

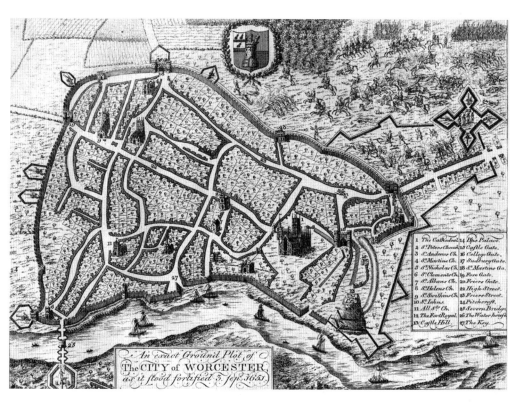

The following legend appears on the map:

1 The Cathedral
2 St Peters Church
3 St Andrews Ch.
4 St Martins Ch.
5 St Nicholas Ch.
6 St Clements Ch.
7 St Albans Ch.
8 St Helens Ch.
9 St Swithins Ch.
10 St Johns
11 All Sts Ch.
12 The Fort Royal
13 Castle Hill
14 The Palace
15 Castle Gate
16 College Gate
17 Sudburygate
18 St Martins Ga.
19 Fore Gate
20 Friers Gate
21 High Street
22 Friers Street
24 Pitchcroft
25 Severn Bridge
26 The Water house
27 The Key

Above: Worcester 1651, Nash.

Right: The house in Worcester from which Charles made his escape after the battle.

Charles as he looked approximately the year before his escape. (van Honthorst)

Lord Wilmot, who was with Charles from the start to the finish of his journey and played a vital role in his escape. (Unattributed engraving)

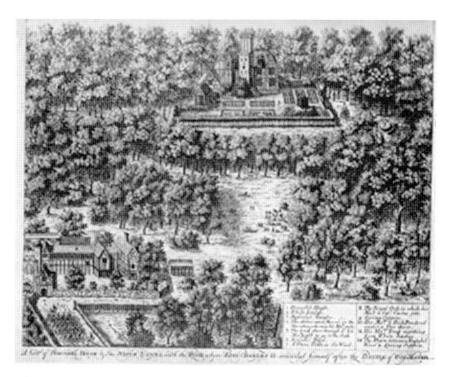

Bird's-eye view of Whiteladies and Boscobel c1660. (From *After Worcester Fight* by Allan Fea)

Boscobel 1798. (From *The Flight of the King*, Allan Fea)

Above left: Priest hole, Boscobel. (From *The Flight of the King*, Allan Fea)

Above right: Isaac Fuller's depiction of Richard Penderel helping Charles into his peasant disguise at Whiteladies.

'Trusty' Richard Penderel, Charles' guide in his attempt to cross the Severn. (Houston)

WILLIAM PENDRILL OF BOSCOBELL IN THE COUNTY OF SALOP ÆTATIS SUÆ 84.

THE ROYALL OAKE

His Face you see. Now breifly heare the Rest;
How well he serv'd his Prince in flight distress't.
Twas, He whose little Houshold did Combine
In Pious Care to save: the Royall Line.
An Oake was thought most safe, for what could prove
More Luckie then the sacred tree to Iove
See where the Hen-roost Ladder stands, by that,
The Mighty Monarch climb'd the Boughs of State,
Where Noble Carlos lent his Manlike Knee,
The last support of Fainting Majestie.
And Natures Tapistrie was the onely shroud
To shelter that Great Prince with Rage pursu'd.

The Nutthook reaching up his Homely fare
Supply'd the want of Waiters standing Bare:
While busie Wife and Children gather wood
To dress the Sheep prepar'd for Better food
Thus many Oakes defend the British Maine
But one preserv'd the British Soveraigne.

Pendrill thy name will shine in History
Brighter then their's, whose Hospittallity
Disguised Deitys hath entertayn'd
For thine was reall t'other Poets faynd.

From the very rare Print in the Possession of A.H. Sutherland Esq̄.

William Penderel, who acted as Charles' barber and helped him into the oak tree. (Unknown artist)

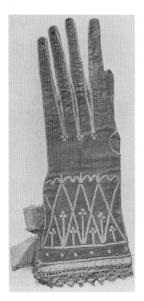

Above left: Glove left by Charles at Whiteladies as a memento. (From *After Worcester Fight*, Allan Fea)

Above right: The bed at Boscobel where Charles slept. (Courtesy Gillian Bagwell)

Left: The lane, as muddy then as when this modern picture was taken, that Charles and Richard Penderel took from Whiteladies to Madeley. (Courtesy Lucy Griffiths)

Evelith Mill at Shifnall, where Charles and Richard Penderel were confronted by the miller. (Courtesy Lucy Griffiths)

The attic at Moseley, where Thomas Whitgreave showed Charles his shrine. (Courtesy Gillian Bagwell)

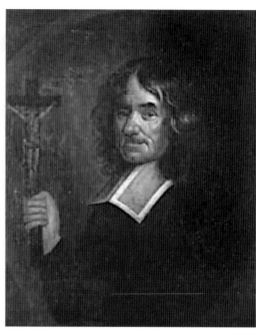

Above left: Thomas Whitgreave of Moseley, who gave sanctuary to Charles. (From *The Flight of the King*, Allan Fea)

Above right: Father John Huddleston. Helped Charles at Moseley and years later ministered to him when he was dying. (Unattributed)

Jane Lane, who rode pillion with Charles for several days. (Artist unknown)

Room at Trent House where Charles slept. (Courtesy Gillian Bagwell)

The inn adjacent to the blackmith's in Bromsgrove. (Courtesy Gillian Bagwell)

The blacksmith's, rear of the Black Cross, Bromsgrove, where the smithy told the disguised king of his hatred for 'that rogue Charles Stuart'. (Courtesey Gillian Bagwell)

The George Inn, Bridport, where Charles brazenly mingled with Roundhead troopers.

The George Inn, Mere where Charles was asked if he was 'a friend of Caesar', i.e. a royalist.

The George Inn, Mere, as it would have looked when Charles visited. (From *The Flight of the King*, Allan Fea)

The same view in the present-day George. (Author's collection)

Queen's Arms, Charmouth, where Charles' fruitless wait for Limbry's boat aroused suspicion. (From *The Flight of the King*, Allan Fea)

Left: The royalist inn the King's Arms, Salisbury, where Wilmot enlisted the help of Colonel Phelips. (From *The Flight of the King*, Allan Fea)

Below: Tattersall's brig the *Surprise*, in which Charles finally escaped to France. (van der Velde)

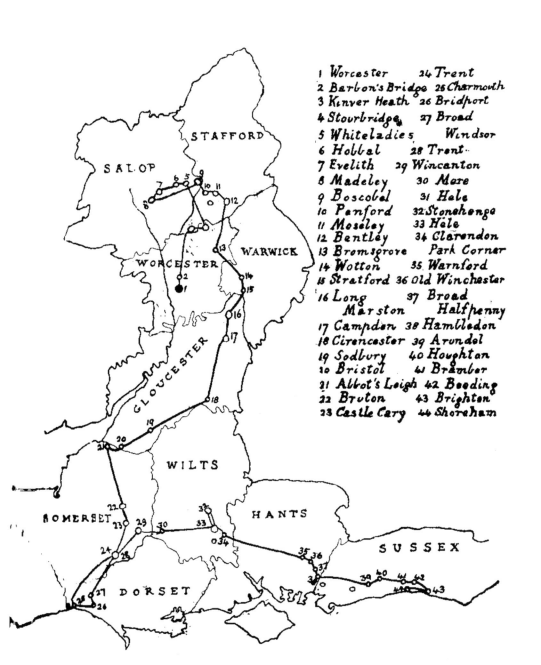

1 Worcester	24 Trent
2 Barton's Bridge	25 Charmouth
3 Kinver Heath	26 Bridport
4 Stourbridge	27 Broad
5 Whiteladies	Windsor
6 Hobbal	28 Trent
7 Evelith	29 Wincanton
8 Madeley	30 More
9 Boscobel	31 Hele
10 Penford	32 Stonehenge
11 Moseley	33 Hele
12 Bentley	34 Clarendon
13 Bromsgrove	Park Corner
14 Wotton	35 Warnford
15 Stratford	36 Old Winchester
16 Long	37 Broad
Marston	Halfpenny
17 Campden	38 Hambledon
18 Cirencester	39 Arundel
19 Sodbury	40 Houghton
20 Bristol	41 Bramber
21 Abbot's Leigh	42 Beeding
22 Bruton	43 Brighton
23 Castle Cary	44 Shoreham

Charles' route from Worcester. (From *The Flight of the King*, Allan Fea)

The Monarch's Way

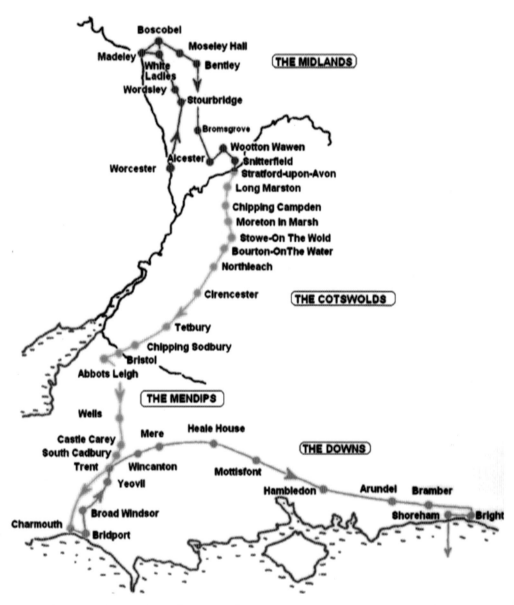

The Monarch's Way long-distance walk. (Courtesy the Monarch's Way Association)

Chapter 13

Bridport

So Frank Windham, and Mrs Coningsby and I, went in the morning, on horse-back, away to Burport; and just as we came into the town, I could see the streets full of red-coats, Cromwell's soldiers...at which Frank Windham was very much startled, and asked me what I would do? I told him, that we must go impudently into the best inn in the town, and take a chamber there, as the only thing to be done... [We] found the yard very full of soldiers. I alighted, and taking the horses thought it the best way to go blundering in among them, and lead them thro' the middle of the soldiers into the stable, which I did; and they were very angry with me for my rudeness.

As soon as we had dined, my Lord Wilmot came into the town from Lyme, but went to another inn. Upon which, we rode out of town, as if we had gone upon the road towards London; and when we were got two miles of, [sic] my Lord Wilmot overtook us, (he having observed, while in town, where we were) and told us, that he believed the ship might be ready next night... Upon which, I not thinking it fit to go back again to the same place where we had sat up the night before, we went to a village called ---- [Broadwindsor].

King Charles, as dictated to Samuel Pepys

Julia Coninsgby rode once again behind Charles as they crossed the river Char to leave Charmouth and laboured up the long, steep and winding road leading towards Bridport, a journey of around seven miles. Arriving in the town, which despite its name was (and is) almost two miles inland, she, Charles and Wyndham soon discovered they were in a quandary, since hundreds of Parliamentary soldiers were in the town, an unmissable red-coated presence on the streets. Julia and Charles had arranged to rendezvous with Wilmot at Bridport's most reputable inn, the George, but there were soldiers there too and this was now looking like a risky proposition. Wyndham came alongside them and asked Charles how he thought they should handle the situation. The king, realizing that this wasn't a search party but just a regiment passing through, boldly decided they should to brazen it out in order to avoid missing Wilmot. They continued their course and rode directly into the yard of the George where the horses would be tended to – and found themselves right in the middle of a large group of soldiers. Julia and Wyndham went inside, leaving Charles with the horses to bluff his way through the Parliamentarians.

*

Horton, the George Inn's ostler, had his hands full. As well as the ordinary visitors he was having to contend with an influx of troopers of Colonel Haynes' regiment, making a stop on their way to a posting in Jersey. And now a new party had arrived on horseback who would need attending to; a gentlewoman riding with her groom, and a gentleman riding alone. After the lady and gentleman had left the servant with their horses and entered the inn, there was a bit of a commotion. The groom had led the horses right through the middle of the soldiers, almost seeming to invite the abuse and complaints that came his way as a result. But the man ignored them, removing the bridle of the horse he had been riding and calling Horton over to him.

He wanted help with his master and mistress' horses and some oats to feed them, which Horton was happy to assist with – but something else had caught the ostler's attention.

'Sure, sir, I know your face... .'

The groom, a tall man with rather dishevelled black hair who looked to be in his early twenties, speculated that Horton knew him from somewhere they had both lived before – where was he from? The ostler explained that he had recently arrived to work here from Exeter, where he had been employed at an inn next door to the home of a merchant called Potter. That must be the answer, the groom exclaimed without hesitation – he had been in Mr Potter's employment for over a year. Now it made sense to Horton:

'Oh! Then I remember you a boy there!' He invited the servant to have a beer with him, but unfortunately the man told Horton that he had to go and wait on his master and get his dinner ready for him. His party were travelling to London and would be back in three weeks, so he would make a point of looking Horton up and sharing a drink with him then.

*

While Charles was attending to the horses in the stables, his 'master' had secured a room and ordered a meal of mutton to be delivered up to them rather than them dining in one of the public rooms. When it arrived, Charles was summoned so that he could eat with them. About this time, Juliana, looking out of the window, noticed Harry Peters riding into the courtyard, and upon being beckoned up he explained that Lord Wilmot had arrived and was refreshing himself and his horse at another inn. The earl's advice was that they should leave Bridport as soon as possible, and he would meet up with them about two miles along the London Road.

*

Captain Macy rode up the West Road towards Bridport from Charmouth at the head of his small group of men and made for the centre of town. When he passed on his news to the authorities, searchers were immediately sent around the town for news of any recent visitors matching the description of the suspects. The information they sought was soon obtained from the George, with the added intelligence that the party in question had left not long ago, heading east on the London road in the direction of Dorchester. Macy gathered his men and set off in pursuit.

*

Lord Wilmot, loitering on his horse at the appointed place on the road between Bridport and Dorchester, finally saw the distant figures of the king and his companions come into view. He believed it might still be possible to persuade Limbry to take them across, so they decided to send Harry Peters to find out. In the meantime, it was far too dangerous to return to Charmouth – and certainly Bridport – and since there was every chance of them being pursued they turned off the London road, heading in a northerly direction and guessing that their new course might take them in the general direction of somewhere like Yeovil or Sherborne.

*

Macy and his men galloped along the Dorchester road. Macy fully expected, based on what he had been told in Bridport, that he must overtake the travellers soon but there was no sign of them and when he reached

Dorchester itself, the story was the same. No one matching their description had been seen in town. It occurred to Macy that he was just a few miles from Pilsdon, where they would find the house of Sir Hugh Wyndham, Frank's uncle. It made sense that they might take refuge there if they were aware of the hue and cry and no longer daring to use the main roads, so that was his next destination. Launching a surprise raid on Pilsdon Manor, Macy became convinced that one young women currently residing there must be Charles wearing a cunning disguise. The females were ignominiously 'investigated' with this theory in mind, but none was found to be the six-foot-plus heir to the throne. The house itself was thoroughly searched, with similarly negative results. Macy skulked back to Charmouth empty handed.

*

When William Ellesdon discovered that the Limbry plan had fallen through and that Charles and his party had disappeared, the temptation of the £1,000 reward money on offer proved too much for him – and he had a pretty good idea of where the king might be found. He galloped over to Pilsdon, about ten miles north of Lyme, where Frank Wyndham's uncle, Sir Hugh, a high court judge was subjected to yet another unwelcomed visitor. Ellesdon brazenly entered the house, telling him that he knew the king was hiding here and demanding that he be surrendered to him. Unsurprisingly, Hugh Wyndham threw Ellesdon out of his house.

*

The long, narrow lane away from the Dorchester road led steeply up towards Bradpole, taking Charles and his travelling companions away from Bridport and inland for about eight miles, until they finally came to a small village and the welcome sight of an inn – another George.

Commentary:

- The Bridport George Inn mentioned isn't the current one on South Street, old though that building looks, but was just round the corner on East Street. At the time of writing it is a charity shop and proudly bears a sign on its frontage declaring that 'King Charles II came here September 23 1651'.
- The road Charles' party took when leaving the London road is Lee Lane. A memorial stone marking this fortuitous change of

direction by Charles was created in 1901 on the 350th anniversary of the event. After leading a somewhat nomadic life, the stone is at the time of writing positioned at the junction of Lee Lane and the modern A35.

- Juliana Coningsby is often described as Anne Wyndham's niece, but genealogists who have tried to confirm this appear to have had little success.

- Like several others involved in the king's escape, Captain Ellesdon applied for a pension as a reward for aiding the escape, but unlike most, he was unsuccessful. It is said that this might be down to Charles' painful memories of the Charmouth debacle, when the ship he was supposed to procure failed to materialise. But that was hardly Ellesdon's fault, and an intervention by Frank Wyndham eventually managed to secure the reward for him. A better reason might be the one given above (as later described by Captain Limbry) which was that Ellesdon tried to betray the king for the reward money.

Chapter 14

Broadwindsor

[I] sent in Peter to know of the merchant, whether the ship would be ready. But the master of the ship, doubting that it was some dangerous employment he was hired upon, absolutely refused the merchant, and would not carry us over. Whereupon we were forced to go back again to Frank Windham's to Trent, where we might be in some safety till we had hired another ship.

King Charles, as dictated to Samuel Pepys

Dusk was closing in when Wilmot and his travelling companions stopped outside the Castle Inn. Frank Wyndham went inside to find out where they were and see if rooms were available. He emerged bearing good news. They were in Broadwindsor, near Beaminster, Dorset. More interestingly, Wyndham informed them that he recognised the landlord as one Rhys Jones, who had once been a servant to an acquaintance of his. He and his wife were Royalists, and they could stay here for the night instead of plodding on in the darkness. However, Wilmot discovered that this stay would require an adjustment to the role-playing by the group. Not only would Charles now be his groom, but Wyndham had decided, for whatever reason, that Wilmot himself was to take the part of his (Wyndham's) brother-in-law, Colonel Bullen Reymes. They would be grateful if their visit could be treated with discretion, Wyndham had told Jones, because of the ban again in force at that time on Royalists travelling beyond five miles from their homes. The most private room Jones could offer them was in the attic – small and with only one bed, but better than nothing.

Now, thanks to Wyndham's hastily concocted story, things started to become complicated for Wilmot. Whether Wyndham knew it or not, Wilmot was soon to discover that Mrs Jones, the landlord's wife, was once the lover of the man whose part he was playing – and when she showed him up to one of the rooms where the party would be staying, she become somewhat 'tactile', and seemed rather keen to rekindle the flame. Wilmot managed to politely rebuff her advances. How long ago this affair had taken place he did not know, but Mrs Jones seemed to readily accept that he was Reymes, other than commenting that he had put some weight on since they had last met.

Unfortunately, neither his nor Charles' worries were quite over for the night, because it wasn't long before soldiers began to flood into Broadwindsor, and forty of them were duly billeted in the Castle. The good news was that once again they weren't a search party after the royal quarry, but, like the troopers at Bridport, were en route to embark for Jersey.

But this development still left Charles' group in a tricky position. Their haven in the attic room kept them away from other guests, but now the soldiers had filled the place to bursting it would be impossible to leave without running the gauntlet of Parliamentarians at close quarters, and in these days of paranoia, soldiers tended to be inquisitive where travellers were concerned.

Luck was on the side of Wilmot, Charles and Juliana Coningsby, however. Not long after the soldiers had piled into the Castle, a pregnant female guest who had been accompanying the soldiers went into labour in the Castle's kitchen. It wasn't a trouble-free process and her agonised shrieks and moans rang through the little inn. Moreover, locals feared that the new arrival would become a burden on their parish – at that time whichever parish a person was born in was responsible for providing relief. A heated and prolonged dispute broke out between the officers of the parish and the soldiers, meaning that all in all the disturbed night ensured that once they did get to sleep it was a sound and lengthy one, allowing Charles and his companions to slip away unnoticed.

*

When Harry Peters met up with Charles' group after returning from Lyme, he brought the news that there was no hope of getting Limbry to take them to France and that the Dorset ports were no longer safe. It was decided that for now they would return to Frank Wyndham's at Trent, while they tried to find an alternative means of escape.

*

Edward Hyde, brother-in-law to Frank Wyndham, was on his way to Trent Court, where he had been invited to dine. His cousin, also Edward (later Lord Clarendon) knew Charles well, having served his father (albeit during the course of a somewhat turbulent relationship with him) and had followed the son to Jersey as his guardian when he was first forced into exile. This Edward had some information which might be of use to His Majesty in his current plight.

Over dinner, he informed his listeners that he was just back from a trip to Salisbury where he had met Robert Phelips, who had served the Royalist cause valiantly as colonel of horse during the war. Phelips was known to Charles, because he had escaped imprisonment and joined Charles' court in exile for a time. Phelips might be useful to them because he had been issued with a 'protection against molestation from the Parliamentary Commissioners'. It was put to Charles that Phelips, able to travel about freely, might be able to help find a boat or ship to carry him to France, and Charles gave his assent to this plan.

*

One morning while Charles was still at Trent, Wyndham was visited by a local tailor who wished to warn him that he had overheard conversations by anti-Royalist locals that 'persons of quality' had taken refuge at Trent Court and that a raid was being planned. Wyndham thanked the tailor for the information but protested that the only person who had recently come to stay was a relative. There was no secrecy involved – and in fact he felt sure that his kinsman would openly accompany him to church for the next service. As soon as the informant had left, Wyndham went to Charles to tell him about the conversation that had taken place, suggesting that he persuade Wilmot to go with him to church in order to quell the rumours – it was obviously far too risky for Charles himself to play the part of his visitor. One thing in their favour was that Wyndham's own pew in the church was positioned in such a way that most people wouldn't be able to get a good view of them. When Charles put it to Wilmot himself, he felt it was a high-risk strategy but reluctantly acceded to it. The church visit went without a hitch and succeeded in quelling the suspicions regarding who was at Trent Court – but it wasn't the last such alarm.

*

Anne Wyndham, Frank's wife, had taken a trip to nearby Sherborne to see if there were any other rumours of Charles being in the vicinity. There were indeed all kinds of vague stories being passed from tongue to tongue, but nothing of any substance. However, when she was about to travel back to Trent that evening, she arrived in time to see a detachment of horsemen arrive in town. To her, there was something furtive in the way they went to their quarters, devoid of the usual fanfare on such occasions, and she was immediately suspicious. Anne delayed her return to Trent Court and instead loitered in the town hoping to overhear some gossip about the new arrivals. Try as she might to pick up any snippet as to what this visit meant, the mystery remained unsolved. She returned home and informed the king of what she'd seen.

Charles made light of the arrival of the troopers, but Anne's instincts caused her to combine forces with Frank to at least persuade the king to inspect the hiding place he would have to use in case of an emergency. This Charles was happy to do and declared that it would serve him perfectly should the need arise.

Nevertheless, Frank Wyndham up sat that night, gazing apprehensively out of the window. His vigil was rewarded when, at around two in the morning, the horsemen mounted up and set off along the road to the coast. He was finally able to get some rest.

*

On the morning of 25 September, Lord Wilmot left Charles at Trent and rode to Salisbury, a journey of around forty miles, to seek Colonel Phelips. With him were his servant, Swan, and the redoubtable Harry Peters. Wilmot also intended to get in touch with John Coventry, a relative of Wyndham and the son of Lord Coventry the Keeper of the Great Seal, who also lived locally.

The most promising place to find people such as these, and the one Frank Wyndham had recommended before Wilmot's departure from Trent, was the King's Arms - appropriately enough, for it was meeting place popular with Royalists. Peters showed Wilmot through the city to St John's Street, and under the archway to the left of the half-timbered frontage into the courtyard at the rear, where their horses could be tended to. Once Wilmot was ensconced in the inn, Peters was dispatched to Coventry's house in the Close and before long brought him to meet the earl. Wilmot explained to Coventry why he was in town and then they sent for Colonel Phelips. Coventry left Wilmot to talk to Phelips privately, slipping away to smoke and chat with Hewett the landlord, and a Royalist supporter.

As Wilmot began to explain himself, Phelips was wary and cautious at first. Wilmot understood – these were dangerous times. However, he decided to go for broke and opened up completely. The king, Wilmot told him, after a long and arduous journey was just a few miles away at Wyndham's house near Sherborne. He urgently needed some sort of vessel to take him to France – could Phelips help?

Phelips was amazed that Charles was hiding out so close to town but didn't hesitate to offer his services. Once all was settled, Coventry was called back, and the group celebrated their new-found fellowship with a few drinks and a few stories from Wilmot about the scrapes and close shaves he and Charles had been through since the Royalist defeat at Worcester.

The following day, a Friday, Colonel Phelips rode to Southampton, a 23-mile journey skirting the edge of the New Forest. He knew a merchant there by the name of Mr Horne – but the man was out so he left a note asking him to meet him the next day at the home of Colonel St Barbe in Broadlands near Romsey, about eight miles to the north.

On the Saturday, Horne duly arrived at Broadlands. Phelips dined with him and after they had eaten, they strolled in the garden of St Barbe's manor house. While they were walking, Phelips asked whether Horne might know of a boat that could transport a couple of friends of his to France. Horne knew of a reliable Southampton man and said he would try to arrange a meeting the following day between the three of them in Redbridge, near the mouth of the river Test to the west of Southampton.

Things were looking promising for Phelips. The meeting went ahead as planned on the Sunday, where he paid the master of the ship £20 in advance, with a promise of a further £20 upon the completion of the mission. The vessel would sail at night in three days' time. The boat was to be ready to sail on the following Wednesday night. After leaving them, Phelips went to the Bear Inn just outside Southampton – but here he learned that the plan had been scuppered before it had even started and once again it was connected with the Parliamentary army's mission to Jersey. The Channel Island was the only remaining Royalist-held territory, and a concerted effort to take it for the Commonwealth was in the offing. Horne and the master of the vessel they had planned to use informed Wilmot that since their discussion it had now commandeered to assist in this assault; it was needed as a transport, taking provisions to the fleet which had taken up station off the coast of Jersey.

Not wishing to remain in the area any longer and risk arousing suspicion, Colonel Phelips rode back to Salisbury. There he discussed the situation with Coventry again, and this time he had with him a Dr Humphrey Henchman, a white haired, white bearded canon of Salisbury Cathedral who had lost his post and estates for aiding Royalists during the war. They turned their attentions to Sussex, the next county along the coast from where they were.

This was because Henchman knew a Colonel George Gounter who lived near Chichester, and felt sure he would be a good man to help them in their quest. But in the meantime, Charles had been at Trent for longer than was expedient, and as an intermediate measure Henchman was able to suggest the home of another staunch Royalist; Mrs Hyde at Heale House, not far from the town of Andover but still nicely secluded.

Commentary:

- The Castle Inn in Broadwindsor is called the George Inn by Allan Fea, but this seems to be a misunderstanding caused by the Castle being destroyed by fire in 1850 and rebuilt as the George Inn. A cottage built on the site is now a listed building, and according to Historic England has on one of its walls a stone tablet bearing the words: King Charles II slept here September 23-24 1651.
- Anne Wyndham's own account implies that the soldiers at the Castle in Broadwindsor were called away before Charles left, whereas Ellesdon in his memoir explicitly states that the disturbances ensured that the soldiers were still snoozing when the royal party departed. I have chosen to follow Ellesdon's version as being the most likely.
- Robert Phelips married Bridget Gorges, daughter of Sir Thomas Gorges, who may well be related to the Dr Thomas Gorges whom Charles met at Abbots Leigh.
- The King's Arms building in Salisbury, near the city's historic Close, still exists and externally probably looks much as it would have done to Charles – but is called the Chapter House at the time of writing. For many years after the events described here, locals said that Hewitt, the landlord of the King's Arms, was a servant at a nearby house used as a hideout by Royalists, and that he acted as a messenger for them and providing warnings when danger was at hand.
- Colonel Gounter is often referred to as Gunter, and in some accounts as Counter.

Chapter 15

Heale

Upon this, I sent further into Sussex, where Robin Philips knew one Colonel Gunter, to see whether he could hire a ship any where upon that coast. And not thinking it convenient for me to stay much longer at Frank Windham's, (where I had been in all about a fortnight, and was become known to very many) I went directly away to a widow gentlewoman's house, one Mrs Hyde… But just as I alighted at the door Mrs Hyde knew me, though she had never seen me but once in her life, and that was with the King, my father, in the army, when we marched by Salisbury, some years before, in the time of the war; but she being a discreet woman took no notice at that time of me, I passing only for a friend of Robin Philips...

While we were at supper, I observed Mrs Hyde and her brother Frederick to look a little earnestly at me, which led me to believe they might know me. But I was not at all startled at it, it having been my purpose to let her know who I was; and accordingly after supper Mrs Hyde came to me, and I discovered myself to her; who told me, she had a very safe place to hide me in, till we knew whether our ship was ready or no. But she said it was not safe for her to trust any body but herself and her sister; and therefore advised me to take my horse next morning, and make as if I quitted the house, and return again about night; for she would order it so that all her servants and everybody should be out of the house, but herself and her sister....

So Robin Philips and I took our horses, and went as far as Stonehenge; and there we staid looking upon the stones for sometime and returned…about the hour she appointed; where I went up into the hiding-hole, that was very convenient and safe, and staid there all alone... After four or five days stay,

HEALE

Robin Philips came to the house, and acquainted me, that a ship was ready provided for me at Shoreham, by Colonel Gunter.

King Charles, as dictated to Samuel Pepys

Charles had been at Trent for nineteen days, the longest he had stayed anywhere since the start of his journey. On Monday, 6 October, Colonel Phelips, along with Harry Peters, took Charles onto the road once more. Their destination was Heale House, home of Mrs Amphillis Hyde, widow of Lawrence Hyde. Phelips had ridden back to Trent the previous day to undertake this task, and as they had before, Charles and Juliana Coningsby rode together. Phelips took them eastward, pausing briefly for a drink and bite to eat at the home of the Royalist, Hussey, passing through Wincanton, and on to Mere with its views across Blackmore Vale into Dorset. The journey from Trent to Heale was to be a long one (at least fifty miles) so another break was taken here, near the southern border of Wiltshire. They walked their horses into the yard of the George Inn on the market square at about midday. Mere had suffered at the hands of the Parliamentarians during the war. The churchyard cross was destroyed, with Parliamentary soldiers said to have been the culprits, while the vicar himself was dragged out of his house, humiliated, beaten and imprisoned. He never quite recovered from his treatment and died a few weeks later. This indicates that the town had Royalist sympathies, and anyway it was a relatively safe place for Charles to stop because Phelips knew Christopher Phillips, the landlord.

Here they ate and talked, and Phillips informed them of the intense activity of the Parliamentarians in trying to find the king in the aftermath of the Battle of Worcester. One story abroad locally was that Charles had reached London in disguise and various houses in the capital had been searched. After the group had eaten, Phillips asked Charles, 'Are you a friend to Caesar?', which the king knew full well to be a coded phrase among Royalist to find out on which side of the fence a stranger stood. When Charles replied that he was indeed a friend to Caesar, the landlord (little knowing that he was talking to 'Caesar' himself) raised his glass, crying, 'Here's a health to the king,' which declaration all present saluted.

Once the party and their horses were rested and refreshed, they embarked upon the final 25-mile trek across Cranborne Chase towards Heale House.

*

Amphillis Hyde was entertaining that night, Thursday, 9 October. There would be her brother-in-law, Frederick Hyde, and Dr Henchman from

Salisbury. And now she was waiting at the door of Heale House, close to the River Avon, to greet her other two guests. It was early evening and getting dark, but she had had advance notification that Colonel Phelips and a friend would be joining them for supper. However, when she saw them approach, even though the light was fading fast she immediately twigged that Phelips wasn't accompanied by any ordinary 'friend'.

Aware that she was not supposed to know who the colonel's companion was, Amphillis tried not to betray her feelings – but she had met Charles and his late father when they had passed through the area during the war. Even though that was a few years ago now and Charles had been little more than a boy, she was in no doubt as to the identity of her visitor.

When supper was over, though, and the chance arose to talk to Charles alone and discreetly, it was Charles himself – seeming to have guessed that Amphillis had recognised him – who made the first move and told her who he was and what kind of mission he was on. She assured the king that there was a good hiding place in the house, but nevertheless felt it would be too risky for him to hang around during the day. His best option would be to find somewhere to take refuge till evening, when the servants wouldn't be around to see him return. She also warned him that it wouldn't be wise to share his secret with anyone else other than her sister and Charles was happy to go along with this advice. The king then left her to talk to Dr Henchman, after which Amphillis' illustrious guest retired for the night.

*

Now, Juliana Coningsby, Charles' second and last Pillion passenger, had, like Jane Lane, done her duty and was free to return to her normal life. Harry Peters was given the task of accompanying her back to her home on Friday, 10 October.

*

On the same day, Robin Phelips rode away from Heale with Charles, pretending that it had been merely an overnight stay and they were moving on. They guided their horses in the direction of Stonehenge, about seven miles to the north. As well as indulging in a leisurely ride around that scenic area, they loitered by the stones themselves, speculating on their purpose and meaning. At dusk, the two men returned and met Henchman in the grounds of Heale House. Luckily for Charles, the Catholic Hydes had long had their own priest-hole, located some distance from the house, and Henchman conducted him to this secret place, where he and Phelips left him to stay the night.

*

Lord Wilmot hadn't followed Charles and Phelips after leaving Salisbury, but as usual went off on a mission of his own. His destination this time was the hamlet of Hinton Daubney in Hampshire, and the home of Lawrence Hyde, the brother-in-law of Amphillis. It was a 50-mile trek, followed by a further ten mile trip to Racton, on the road to Chichester: his task was to find out whether the Royalist Colonel Gounter could help in procuring a boat.

*

Colonel George Gounter's family had lived at Racton for centuries, and George himself had commanded a regiment of horse during the war. He had been out, and it was about 8 o'clock when he returned home to be informed by his wife that he had a visitor. It was a Devonshire gentleman sent by Mr Hyde on a very private matter, and he was waiting in the parlour.

When Gounter followed his wife to their parlour to see who might be there, he saw a figure sitting by the fire, rising to greet him. As soon as he did so, a glimmer of recognition leapt into his mind – this guest was Lord Wilmot. Observing his expression, Wilmot drew Gounter away a little while his wife remained by the fire.

'I see you know me,' said the visitor quietly. 'Do not own me.'

Gounter invited Wilmot to take some sack with him while they talked privately and gradually got to hear Wilmot's story. Gounter was eager to assist and offered to make a trip to Chichester to sound out a merchant called Francis Mansel. In the meantime, Wilmot was invited to spend the night at Racton.

During the night, his lordship's sleep was disturbed by the appearance at his bedroom door of his host in the flickering light of the candle he held to guide his way. Gounter explained that his wife was worried, concerned that something dangerous was afoot between the two men and had been plying him with questions about who their mystery visitor was and what their hushed conversations were about. Gounter had only felt able to beg her to trust him, explaining that she herself was in no danger. This enigmatic and rather ominous reply had only upset her further – so now here he was, seeking Wilmot's advice. Gounter stressed that he trusted his wife to keep any secret implicitly, but he would tell her nothing unless Wilmot gave his assent. This Wilmot did and Gounter was able to return to his room and acquaint his wife with the full story.

Colonel Gounter set off early on the morning of Wednesday, 8 October, with his servant John Day. Day knew a few sailors at Emsworth, which was on a little inlet used by small vessels just a few miles south of Racton. But try as they might, there was nothing suitable that could be hired. Gounter returned to tell Wilmot and together they went to try their luck further west at Langstone, another little harbour where boats of the kind they sought might be found. It was the same story. All they could do was partake in a quick meal of fresh oysters before going their separate ways. It was a wet and windy night by the time Wilmot headed back to see Hyde at Hinton Daubney. Gounter, meanwhile, went home to make further enquires.

George Gounter slept for just a couple of hours before setting forth once more. First, he rode to Chichester, where he sounded out his cousin, Captain Thomas Gounter, who had been making enquiries on his behalf, but this also proved to be a dead-end. Then another promising Chichester name came to him…

*

Sitting having a quiet drink in a Chichester hostelry, merchant Francis Mansel saw a man making his way over to his table whom he knew by sight but not by name. This man sidled up and introduced himself, asking Mansel if he wouldn't mind joining him. Before long, they were toasting each other with French wine and puffing on Spanish tobacco. After a time, Mansel's new acquaintance said he had a favour to ask.

'I have two special friends who have been engaged in a duel and there is mischief done. I am obliged to get them off if I can.'

Might Mansel know, he asked, who he could turn to to arrange passage to France on a small trading ship? Such was the urgent nature of this matter that a payment of £50 was available for success. Mansel felt fairly confident that he knew just where to look. He wasn't able to go that day but promised Gounter that they would meet again in the morning and go together. Gounter reported back to Wilmot, finally able to bring some rather more positive news.

*

On Friday, 10 October, Nicholas Tattersal, master of the *Surprise*, a 34 ton coal brig, was sailing his vessel to Chichester along the south coast from his home port of Brightelmstone, when he put in at Shoreham.

Here he was approached by someone bearing a note from Francis Mansel requesting that they meet the next day: Saturday, October 11. It sounded important.

Tattersal duly arrived at the inn where Mansel was staying. He discovered that there was another man with him who stayed in the background, saying little. Tattersal was told the story of the friends who had been involved in a fatal duel and were very keen to flee the country before the authorities could catch up with them. Tattersal was available and certainly interested. Now, Tattersal heard the previously taciturn second man become properly involved for the first time. Mansel's companion explained that he couldn't say for sure exactly when the two duellists would be able to get to the coast to set sail, but time was of the essence. If Tattersal would put himself on standby, ready to sail at an hour's notice, the speaker would personally cover any costs incurred. After some negotiations, a main payment of £60 was settled upon, which was independent of the reimbursement of expense as guaranteed by the second man. Handshakes were exchanged, and the three men departed the inn.

*

Lord Wilmot was paying a social visit to Anthony Brown, a relative of Gounter and a tenant of Mr Hyde's who lived nearby in Hinton Daubney. It was late in the evening when Wilmot got the news he had wanted to hear. George Gounter, who arrived in company with Robin Phelips, whom he had picked up from Hyde's house along the way, was able to report that a ship and its master had been found and it looked like they might finally be able to smuggle His Majesty out of the country. Their contact in Brighthelmstone had proved amenable to their approach, but they must move quickly. Gounter had been on the go for many hours with little sleep and Wilmot could see it, so he chose Robin Phelips to go to tell the king, still at Heale, to be ready to leave. The final, and most dangerous, phase of the whole odyssey was about to begin.

*

It was the early hours of the morning of Sunday, 12 October and Robin Phelips was leading both his and King Charles' horse to the rendezvous spot – the gate which led from Hyde's land to the banks of the River Avon. The appointed hour was 3 am. But as he passed through the gate grasping the bridle of Charles' horse, it broke and the animal, somewhat spooked, dashed away from him along the riverside. It took Phelips some time to catch up with and get hold of the horse, but he eventually managed it and effected a temporary repair to the bridle. Phelips and the king set off into the dark autumnal night.

Commentary:

- Juliana Coningsby, Colonel Wyndham's cousin, was rewarded with a pension for her role in Charles' escape 'as often promised'.
- Henchman went on to serve as Bishop of Salisbury and also London. After the Great Fire in 1666, he was consulted extensively by Wren on the restoration of St Paul's, and contributed financially to the project.
- In later years, Brighthelmstone officially adopted the shortened, informal version of its name that the locals had been using for many years – Brighton.
- Tattersal's name was sometimes spelt 'Tattershall' and occasionally 'Tettersell'.

Chapter 16

Brighton

At two o'clock in the morning, I went out of the house by the back-way, and, with Robin Philips, met Colonel Gunter and my Lord Wilmot together, some fourteen or fifteen miles off, on my way towards Shoreham and were to lodge that night at a place called Hambleton [Hambledon] because it was too long a journey to go in one day to Shoreham. And here we lay at a house of a brother-in-law of Colonel Gunter's… where I was not to be known, (I being still in the same gray-cloath suit, as a serving-man) though the master of the house was a very honest poor man, who, while we were at supper, came in, he having been all the day playing the good-fellow at an ale-house in the town, and taking a stool sat down with us; where his brother-in-law, Colonel Gunter, talking very feelingly concerning Cromwell, and all his party, he went and whispered his brother in the ear, and asked, whether I was not some round-headed rogue's-son?

King Charles, as dictated to Samuel Pepys

On the afternoon of Monday, 13 October, Colonel Gounter went out riding with his cousin Thomas, and Lord Wilmot. Gounter left them for a time to travel to his sister's house in Hambledon and persuaded her to let him have the use of her pack of dogs because he was going out hare coursing with his friends. Accordingly, Gounter and the others, along with Lord Wilmot's man Peters, set off with their animals out onto the South Downs. In fact, there was to be no coursing and their destination was a hill known as Old Winchester – this was where they had arranged to meet Charles and Phelips.

But once they were there, the time for their meeting came and went and the little welcoming committee began to worry that something had gone wrong. Colonel Gounter eventually decided to ride down the slope and explore along the road Charles would probably be taking on his journey from Heale. He had ventured nearly three miles and was on the outskirts of the village of Warnford when he saw Charles and Phelips heading towards them. However, there were houses and people about here and, other than giving them a meaningful look, Gounter played it safe and ignored them, letting them pass while he continued into the village so as not to arouse suspicion. Now that he was committed to entering Warnford, he did what many travellers would do and called at the local inn for a beer and a smoke of his pipe.

Gounter finally caught up with Charles and the others at the Old Winchester rendezvous spot and they were soon underway. As they travelled, Gounter told Charles that the proposed place for tonight's stay was the home of Lawrence Hyde in Hinton Daubney, where they were ready to receive His Majesty. However, Charles felt that place might be too conspicuous and suggested they find somewhere less grand and likely to attract interest by the authorities. By now, they were not far from Hambledon where Gounter's sister Ursula lived. It wouldn't come as too much of a shock to her, because this was where he had obtained the hunting dogs, and as a precaution he had mentioned to her that he might call in with some friends later. Charles was comfortable with this plan, so Gounter led them to her long, low cottage on the outskirts of the quaint village which lay in the Forest of Bere.

*

Having been forewarned of such a possibly, Ursula Symons wasn't too surprised to have her humble home invaded just as it was getting dark by the small group of men returned from a day's coursing in the country. She had a good fire going in the parlour, and served up wine, ale and biscuits to her guests.

While they were dining, Ursula's husband Thomas arrived home.

'This is brave,' he declared good naturedly. 'A man can no sooner be out of the way but his house must be taken up with I know not whom!' Then he turned to Gounter. 'Is it you?' he said, finally recognising the colonel in the flickering light from the fire and candles. 'You are welcome, and, as your friends, so are they all.'

Things took a slightly trickier turn as they ate, when Thomas's gaze finally fell on Charles properly for the first time and examined his crudely cut short hair.

'Here is a Roundhead,' he declared to Gounter. 'I never knew you keep Roundheads' company before.'

'It is no matter. He is my friend, and I will assure you no dangerous man.'

Thomas Symons moved to place himself down in a chair next to Charles and held out his hand to shake. 'Brother Roundhead, for his sake thou art welcome.'

At Symons' insistence the drink was flowing freely, but this was causing Gounter some concern. Apart from not wanting Charles to become so intoxicated as to risk giving the game away, there was the small matter of a very long – and vital – day ahead tomorrow. When they could do so without Symons noticing, Gounter and the others relieved Charles of whatever drink he had in his hand and when it came to around ten o'clock, Gounter cleverly played on Symons' notion that Charles was a Roundhead by whispering to him that they would be able to relax and enjoy themselves more if they sent him to bed early. Symons was only too happy to go along with this plot.

*

The next morning, Colonel Robert Phelips bade farewell to the king, Wilmot and Gounter, receiving Charles' heartfelt thanks before he went. His immediate work was accomplished and Gounter would take over from here. But there was still work to be done, because Phelips now took the London road, where his task was to secure funds for when Charles – should all go according to plan – arrived in France.

*

> The Council of State to the Customs' Officers of all the ports of England. Council has informations inducing probabilities that Charles Stuart is still in England… obscured and under disguise, expecting a fit time to pass into foreign parts. Have a special care of that which is otherwise your duty, and use your utmost diligence to make a strict search, and take due consideration of all such as attempt to pass beyond the seas from your port, or any creek, and suffer none to pass whom you may have cause to suspect to be Charles Stuart… We need not put you in mind that Parliament has appointed 1,000l to be given to him or them that shall apprehend the leader of the later invading army.
>
> For your better discovery of him, take notice of him to be a tall man, above two yards high, his hair a deep brown near to black, and has been, we hear, cut off since the destruction of his army at Worcester, so that it is not very long; expect him under disguise, and do not let any pass without a due and

particular search, and look particularly to the bye creeks and places of embarkation in or belonging to your port.

Whitehall Oct. 14th

*

Early on Tuesday, 14 October, George Gounter led Charles and Wilmot towards Brighton. They stopped for refreshments at a cottage in Racton, Gounter's home village, and moved on. Crossing the Downs, perhaps catching a distant glimpse of Chichester Cathedral, they neared Arundel. Here they came upon a potential danger to their plans. Gounter recognised in the distance the governor of Arundel Castle, Captain Morley, out hunting with a group of his men. To make themselves less conspicuous, Gounter and the rest dismounted, leaving the path and leading their horses down the hill. He took them on a slight detour northwards in the direction of Houghton, where once more they allowed themselves a short break (Charles didn't even dismount) before crossing the nearby River Arun. At the inn there, Gounter gave Charles a couple of 'neat' tongues (cow tongues, usually dried and preserved) a common food item then which he'd brought with him from the Symons' house.

Pressing on eastward, the next leg of the journey took them into Bramber, where once again they encountered Parliamentary soldiers milling about on both sides of the street. They were already in full view of the Parliamentarians before they had time to react, but Wilmot was all for turning back. Gounter counselled keeping their nerve.

'If we do, we are undone. Let us go on boldly, and we shall not be suspected.

'He sayeth well,' agreed Charles.

Consequently, they employed the same audacious approach that had worked for Charles in the courtyard of the George at Bridport, but with Gounter leading and Charles behind, and successfully continued right past the troopers as if unconcerned. Fortunately for them, the troops were 'off-duty', coming into the village to take refreshments after a stint guarding the nearby bridge.

Later the same afternoon, though, it seemed that their plan might have backfired – Charles alerted Gounter that the troops from Bramber were now quickly coming up behind them. Had someone recognised them? They slowed, hoping to allow the forty or so riders to pass – which thankfully they did, jostling them roughly in the narrow lane as they did so, but disappearing into the distance.

But this second encounter had unsettled Wilmot. Gounter was taking them to the house of a Mr Backshall, where they could rest and refresh themselves while the colonel undertook a reconnaissance mission to see that the coast was clear. But the earl, perhaps understandably spooked, insisted on leading Charles off the main road and across country. Gounter continued on his way, and, after a long day's riding a further ten miles took him to the little fishing village of Brighthelmstone and the George Inn, where he waited to hear that his companions had arrived safely.

Commentary:

- There is a cottage in Hambledon called 'The King's Rest' which locals identify as the home of Ursula Symonds, sister of Colonel Gounter, where Charles stayed. But Allan Fea in his authoritative *Flight of the King* says that the original house was demolished in the eighteenth century, and describes foundations that could still be seen on the ground. He also mentions outbuildings still standing, which may account for the current 'King's Rest' – but he categorically states that they weren't built till 1720, 'therefore having no connection with our story'.

- Charles later gave Ursula and Thomas Symons a punchbowl, ladle, and drinking cups embellished with the royal coat of arms. (One wonders how Thomas reacted when he discovered the true identity of the 'Roundhead' whose company he had been so keen to escape.)

- Two years after his part in helping Charles, Phelips was arrested and imprisoned in the Tower of London. Men were sent to the house where his wife was then living, and her belongings were searched for incriminating evidence. Eventually, she was given permission to join her husband at the Tower, but before she could do so Phelips himself staged an escape from captivity and managed to smuggle himself aboard a ship bound for France, where he rejoined Charles. When the king returned to England in triumph, Phelips was well rewarded financially, as well as being appointed to the posts of Groom of the King's Bedchamber and Chancellor of the Duchy of Lancaster.

- Some authorities also dispute whether Charles did stop at Racton where Gounter lived.

- A similar dampener is put on the local story that Charles stopped at a pub in Houghton called the George and Dragon, because Fea says that 'the present little inn is comparatively modern'.
- Sadly, Colonel George Gounter died not long after these events at the age of about sixty, leaving his wife struggling financially. She petitioned Charles shortly after the Restoration describing herself as being in a 'desperate condition'. On her husband's death she had inherited massive debts, largely incurred by the colonel while trying to help Charles' escape. The king saw to it that she received a pension, and later arranged for one of her sons to attend Oxford University.
- At this stage, the Commonwealth government still had little idea of how far Charles had progressed in his escape. As late as 13 October a message was sent north to Captain Ley: 'There are strong probabilities that Charles Stuart and the Duke of Buckingham were in or about Staffordshire some days after the victory at Worcester, and probably they may still be in those parts under disguise... .'
- 'Roundhead' was originally a derogatory term and derived from the short or cropped hairstyles of many Puritans.

Chapter 17

Departure

So when we came to the inn at Bright-helmstone, we met with one [Mansel] the merchant, who had hired the vessel, in company with her master, the merchant only knowing me, as having hired her only to carry over a person of quality, that was escaped from the battle of Worcester... I observed that the master of the vessel looked very much upon me. And as soon as we had supped, calling the merchant aside, the master told him, that he had not dealt fairly with him; for though he had given him a very good price for the carrying over that gentleman, yet he had not been clear with him; for, says he, he is the King, and I very well know him to be so...for he took my ship, together with other fishing vessels at Bright-helmstone, in the year 1648, (which was when I commanded the King my father's fleet, and I very kindly let them go again.) But, says he to the merchant, be not troubled at it; for I think I do God and my country good service, in preserving the King, and, by the grace of God, I will venture my life and all for him, and set him safely on shore, if I can, in France…

And here I also run another very great danger…for as I was standing, after supper, by the fire-side, leaning my hand upon a chair, and all the rest of the company being gone into another room, the master of the inn came in, and fell a talking with me, and just as he was looking about, and saw there was nobody in the room, he, upon a sudden, kissed my hand that was upon the back of the chair, and said to me, God bless you wheresoever you go; I do not doubt, before I die, but to be a lord, and my wife a lady: so I laughed, and went away into the next room… there being no remedy against my being known by him…

About four o'clock in the morning, myself and the company beforenamed went towards Shoreham…and came to the vessel's side, which was not above sixty tun. But it being low water, and the vessel lying dry, I and my Lord Wilmot got up with a ladder into her, and went and lay down in the little cabbin, till the tide came to fetch us off. But I was no sooner got into the ship, and lain down upon the bed, but the master came in to me, fell down upon his knees, and kist my hand; telling me, that he knew me very well, and would venture life, and all that he had in the world, to set me down safe in France.

So about five o'clock in the afternoon, as we were in sight of the Isle of Wight, we stood directly over to the coast of France, the wind being then full north; and the next morning, a little before day, we saw the coast. But the tide failing us, and the wind coming about to the south-west, we were forced to come to an anchor, within two miles of the shore, till the tide of flood was done.

We found ourselves just before an harbour in France, called Fescamp; and just as the tide of ebb was made, espied a vessel to leeward of us, which, by her nimble working, I suspected to be an Ostend privateer. Upon which, I went to my Lord Wilmot, and telling him my opinion of that ship, proposed to him our going ashore in the little cock-boat... The master also himself had the same opinion of her being an Ostender, and came to me to tell me so, which thought I made it my business to dissuade him from, for fear it should tempt him to set sail again with us for the coast of England; yet so sensible I was of it, that I and my Lord Wilmot went both on shore in the cock-boat; and going up into the town of Fescamp, staid there all day to provide horses for Rouen. But the vessel which had so affrighted us, proved afterwards only a French hoy.

King Charles, as dictated to Samuel Pepys

Gounter was relieved to find that neither Brighthelmstone nor the George were infested with the seemingly ubiquitous Parliamentary troopers, and the inn itself was quiet. He booked the best room and had just settled down to enjoy a glass of wine when Gaius Smith the landlord popped his head round the door.

'More guests!'

Smith showed them to another room. Gounter pretended not to take any notice, but observed that it was indeed Charles and Wilmot, accompanied by Mansel the merchant and Tattersal the master of the *Surprise*. Eventually, Gounter tentatively approached the room where the men were chatting, and, in the presence of Smith, he heard a voice from within:

'Here, Mr Barlow, I drink to you!' Gunter knew it was Charles, addressing Wilmot and giving Gounter his cue.

'I know that name,' Gounter told the landlord. 'I pray enquire whether he was not a major in the king's army.'

Gounter went through the charade of entering their room and asking if this were true, and upon receiving a positive reply, invited them to join him for a drink – his room being the larger of the two.

Later, at supper, Gounter was surprised by how calm and even cheerful Charles appeared. They were entering the endgame and there was still time for things to go badly wrong (as they had discovered at Lyme Regis) yet the young king had maintained such a composed demeanour all the time that Gounter had been with him.

*

Gaius Smith the landlord had been waiting on the new visitors and their friends during the evening. Gaius had a good memory, and he now was sure that he knew who one of them was.

He kept it to himself all evening, but there came a point where he could contain himself no longer. The tall friend of 'Mr Barlow' was leaning with a hand on the back of a chair, warming his back against the fire, and Gaius approached him, knelt, and kissed the hand that was resting on the chair back.

'It shall not be said but I have kissed the best hand in England. God bless you wheresoever you go. I do not doubt before I die, but to be a lord and my wife a lady.'

Charles laughed this off, and wandered back to the other room.

*

When Gounter joined Charles, he was full of concern about the king's embarrassing encounter with Smith. He tried to assure Charles that he had no idea how the servant could have known who he really was.

'Peace, peace, Colonel,' Charles said. 'The fellow knows me, and I him. He was one that belonged to the back-stairs to my father. I hope he is an honest fellow.'

Reassured, Gounter then went to Tattersal, eager to know when they might be able to sail. The answer wasn't promising. To aid the secrecy of their mission he had moved his barque from Brighthelmstone harbour to a creek further along the coast, but with the tide currently being out, the vessel was grounded. Another thing that had been against them was the wind, which had been blowing onto the shore; but just then Charles, opening a window to check on the weather, found that the wind had turned. Gounter tried offering the master an extra £10 to leave that night, as soon as the ship might be afloat, but he stuck to his guns. He did at least agree to begin the process of manning his ship during the night so that it would be ready to weigh anchor first thing in the morning.

Now came a further hiccup. First, Tattersal suddenly demanded more money, talking of the need to insure his ship. Considering that he already knew what the voyage entailed and was an experienced seaman, this was a very flimsy and transparently greedy ploy. Gounter, Charles and Wilmot argued the point, reminding him of the agreement they had already made. Tattersal didn't back down, and in fact named his price: £200. They had little choice but to accept. Next, Tattersal wanted a 'bond', that is, Gounter must put the promise of the extra payment into writing. The exasperated colonel had had enough. Tattersal's ship wasn't the only one on the south coast, and if the master refused to fulfil his side of the bargain they would go elsewhere.

Seeing that the argument was getting heated, Charles himself now intervened.

'He sayeth right,' the king assured Tattersal. Colonel George Gounter was a gentleman, and as such his word – especially when uttered in front of witnesses – was as good as his bond. Thankfully, Tattersal conceded at least this point. It was finally agreed that the embarkation time would be 2 in the morning and to demonstrate his reliability, he swore that he would sink his ship rather than allow it to be taken, should they be discovered. (Whether Charles, as a prospective passenger, found this prospect particularly comforting isn't recorded.) They kept Tattersal drinking and talking for as long as they could, keen to keep him away from his wife or anyone else who might try to talk him out of it and thus avoid a repeat of the debacle with Limbry, till eventually it was time for him to leave and make his preparations. Gounter stayed awake 'on watch', while Charles and Wilmot, fully clothed, tried to get some sleep.

*

Tattersal finally returned home to prepare for the voyage, telling his wife that he had been told his ship had broken her moorings and he needed to go and attend to it. His wife, however, had cottoned on to what was happening – but unlike Mrs Limbry, she was prepared to share the risk of discovery if it meant saving the king's life.

*

Gounter checked his pocket watch then nudged Charles and Wilmot and showed them the timepiece. The hour had come. The little group slipped out of the George, mounted their horses and rode to the creek where Tattersal had moored his brig. This time, everything had gone to plan and Tattersal, his crew of five and his ship were waiting and ready to sail. The wind was fair, and all they could do now was board and then wait for the tide.

This was where Gounter took his leave of his king. It was time for him to return to his family, but he expressed the hope to Charles that he had done his best, and that any mistakes he had made were through 'error, not want of good will or loyalty'. Charles and Wilmot said their farewells and gave their thanks for all he had done. Then the king and Wilmot climbed up the side of the currently beached *Surprise* and retired to a cabin. It was better for them to be out of sight because the conditions weren't right for sailing yet and there was still time for them to be ambushed. For that reason, Gounter's last act for his king was to remain at the beach till the tide turned with the horses in case of a late emergency.

Finally, at between seven and eight o'clock on Wednesday, 15 October, the little ship nosed her way out of the creek and into the open sea. Gounter stood watching from the shore till she was over the horizon, then led the horses away.

*

When morning came in Brighthelmstone Parliamentary soldiers poured into the village, seeking a black-haired man, six-feet two inches tall. There was no one of that description to be found.

*

Tattersal had put it about that he was delivering coal to Poole – even his crew were still under this impression – so the *Surprise* initially headed west along the coast. The captain was still worrying about the dangers of being implicated in this affair and how they might get to France without incurring any more risk than was necessary. He didn't want to tell his crew the real story, so as they approached the Isle of Wight, he quietly asked Charles to act out a little charade. Tattersal suggested that the king concoct a story which might persuade his men to divert to France before they went to unload their coal.

He waited while Charles obligingly addressed the little crew, spinning a version of the cover story that Limbry had used, that he and Wilmot were two merchants who had unluckily run up debts in England and were in danger of being arrested – but that they had money owing to them in Rouen, in France. If only the crew could persuade the master to make a detour to Dieppe or any port near Rouen, he and his companion would be so grateful that they would reward them with drinking money amounting to twenty shillings. The wind was, after all, very fair for such a journey.

The four men and one boy who made up the crew certainly liked the sound of this and tried to persuade their captain. Tattersal played his part as well as Charles, humming and hawing and complaining that it would take him out of his way. Eventually, though, he allowed the combined pleadings of the crew, together with Charles and Wilmot when they joined in, to persuade him. At about 5 o'clock, with the Isle of Wight in sight, Tattersal ordered the ship's head turned to the south, and France.

*

Later, while Tattersal was chatting to the king, one of his seamen, who was standing upwind of them puffing on his pipe. The smoke was blowing into Charles' face, and Tattersal asked him to move to some other place on the ship.

"Why, a cat may look at a king, surely!' grumbled the seaman.

*

The *Surprise* sailed through the night under an almost full moon, until, just as it was getting light, Wilmot saw the French coast in the distance. But the tide and wind conspired to keep them from making a landing, so Tattersal ordered the lowering of the anchor about two miles from shore off Fécamp, between Dieppe and Le Havre. As Wilmot gazed on this welcome sight, so tantalisingly close yet still out of reach, Charles came to his side with troubling news. A vessel had sailed into view to the leeward of the *Surprise*, and the king was worried that it could be a privateer. France was at that time at war with Spain, and Charles' fear was not just that they might be robbed, but that the privateers might release their English captives in their home country after taking their vessel. Tattersal himself believed the mystery ship to be a privateer, but Charles quietly told Wilmot that he had openly poo-pooed the idea in case he took fright and turned his ship about to flee back to England. It eventually became clear that the distant vessel had no interest in the *Surprise*, and between them, Wilmot and Charles persuaded Tattersal to lower the ship's boat and put them ashore rather than wait for the conditions to allow the ship to weigh anchor and enter the harbour. Crewmen rowed their passengers to the beach, and one of Tattersal's sailors carried Charles on his back through the surf to dry land and safety.

When mention is made of how arduous Charles' six week flight from Worcester to the south coast was, it's easy to forget that even that it isn't the whole story. The young king had already travelled 300 miles from Scotland, fought a bloody battle, then fled that same night as a hunted man to endure a further 400-plus miles of hiding, backtracking, and dodging an ever-present enemy.

The danger was over, but it was the start of a period of exile that was to last nine years.

Commentary:

- The King's Head is often claimed as the pub occupying the site of the George, where Charles met Tattersal, but the antiquary Frederick Sawyer's research found no trace of any George Inn in West Street before 1754. There was one on Middle Street, and 'this, there can be little doubt, was the place visited by the King'.
- I know of no actual evidence to substantiate the common claim that Tattersal recognised the king, and that this is why he tried to go back on his initial arrangement to make the journey for £60. I doubt whether Tattersal did actually recognise Charles, and think it possible that Gaius Smith – who certainly did know Charles – had found it impossible to resist gossiping and it reached Tattersal's ears.
- Local tradition has it that Tattersal's ship was moored at – and the king's departure took place from – the mouth of the River Adur, and this certainly seems the most likely spot. A 2001 discussion on the website of the British Marine Life Study Society reported that 'The current view is that he did not leave from Shoreham as we know it, but from the area now occupied by Hove lagoon, nearer the mouth of the Adur as it was then' (https://www.glaucus.org.uk/Surprise.htm).
- The Cromwellian soldiers who came searching for Charles shortly after his departure may have caused Mansel, the

merchant who had put Gounter in touch with Tattersal, to flee for his life, because he was another of the many petitioners to the king once Charles was back in England and established on the throne. Mansel was granted a pension, but the diarist Samuel Pepys chanced to meet him at the Leg in King Street in 1667. Poor Mansel hadn't been paid his pension for several years and was destitute, 'ready to starve' and 'looking after getting of a prizeship to live by'. Mansel, a thriving merchant before becoming embroiled in rescuing Charles, also provided Pepys with an insight into those events: 'He told me several particulars of the King's coming thither, which was mighty pleasant, and shews how mean a thing a king is, how subject to fall, and how like other men he is in his afflictions'.

- Soon after the Restoration, the *Surprise* sailed up the Thames and was anchored near Whitehall as a kind of tourist attraction. It was subsequently renamed the *Royal Escape* and was adopted as a royal yacht by Charles. In one of the many coincidences that abound in this story, the ship had been intercepted for some reason by a royal squadron a few years before Worcester, and Charles himself, then the Prince of Wales, had intervened to see that she was allowed to continue on her journey. This is supposed to be how Tattersal recognised Charles, but as I say, there doesn't seem to be any concrete proof to back this up. (And whether Charles realised that they were one and the same vessel also isn't recorded.) Charles was surprisingly magnanimous towards Tattersal, considering his sneaky last-minute ploy to obtain almost four times the payment he had agreed to, because the king treated him well after the Restoration. He was provided with a good pension and made a captain in the Royal Navy. He was also among the party attending the king when he made his triumphant from Holland to reclaim his throne.

But the life of a naval officer didn't last long, and after a couple of years Tattersal returned to his old lifestyle, before ending his days as the landlord of the Old Ship Hotel. When he died in 1674 at around sixty years of age, he was buried at St Nicholas' in Brighton, where his comparatively grand tombstone, hard by the south wall of the church, declared that 'he preserved the Church, the Crown, and the Nation'. It may be, though, that Tattersal's determination to squeeze more money out of Charles' predicament perhaps indicates a darker side to his nature. There are some indications that he was, in fact, dismissed from the navy 'for his behaviour during a naval engagement'. As well as being given command of at least two navy ships, he was made High Constable of Brighton, and according to John A. Bishop in *A Peep into the Past* (1880) he is said to have exercised his powers 'with the zeal of a bigot and the malign industry of a ministerial spy'. Among other things, on one occasion he and his officers broke down the door of a house where he believed (based on no more evidence than claiming to hear 'an elevated tone of prayer or instruction') that a Quaker meeting was taking place, and managed to secure a conviction.

After one of Tattersal's sailors – Richard Carver – died at around the time of the Restoration, his widow wrote to Charles for assistance, pointing out that Carver turned down the chance to get the £1,000 reward for reporting him to the authorities. It wasn't money she was after, but 'the liberation of some of his friends, the Quakers, which was not granted him' (so it sounds as if Carver died in jail for his faith). There is no record of whether any Quakers were released at this time, but a few years later Charles agreed to an interview with the mate of the *Surprise* – the man who carried him ashore when they reached France. He made a similar request, and the king agreed to six Quakers being granted their freedom.

- After putting Charles and Wilmot ashore, a storm came on which obliged Tattersal to cut the ship's cable and put some distance between himself and the coast, thus causing him to lose his anchor. He duly charged this to Gounter upon his return, obliging the colonel to cough up a further £8.

Chapter 18

Freedom

The next day we got to Rouen, to an inn, one of the best in the town, in the Fish-market, where they made difficulty to receive us, taking us, by our cloaths, to be some thieves, or persons that had been doing some very ill thing, until Mr Sandburne, a merchant, for whom I sent, came and answered for us. We staid at Rouen one day to provide ourselves better cloaths, and give notice to the Queen, my mother, (who was then at Paris) of my being safely landed. After which, setting out in a hired coach, I was met by my mother, with coaches, short of Paris; and by her conducted thither, where I safely arrived.

King Charles, as dictated to Samuel Pepys

John Samborne was a wealthy English Royalist merchant who had fled to France and settled in Rouen, along with his brother Thomas, to avoid having his properties sequestered by the state. On the morning of Friday, 17 October, he received an unexpected summons to visit an inn in the fish market and see a fellow Englishman there who was having some trouble convincing the owners that he was a respectable person who would be able to pay his way. When Samborne arrived, he discovered that it was not just any Englishman but King Charles himself, having ridden with Wilmot from a disembarkation point at Fécamp – yet in such an unkempt and shady-looking state that the landlord of the inn was none too keen to allow him to stay.

Samborne had had dealings with both Charles and his father in the past, having spent over £25,000 of his own money on ammunition and other supplies during the struggles of both monarchs, including being involved in various schemes to try to restore the young king to his throne. It's not surprising, then, that Charles confided to Samborne that he was the 'first and only man he could trust' in this place and naturally, the latter was eager to help. The merchant sorted out some decent clothing (keeping some of the tattered apparel the king removed as souvenirs) and saw to it that he had no trouble from the innkeeper. Samborne's final task was to go ahead of Charles to Paris and take a packet bearing the news of her son's arrival to Henrietta Maria. Before leaving, he introduced Charles to another merchant, one William Scott, and in fact Charles soon transferred from the inn to Scott's house, where he and Wilmot stayed for a few days. Scott, like Samborne, provided Charles with funds for when he moved on to Paris. It might seem surprising that someone of his status would need such help, but Royalist exiles abroad were all financially embarrassed to some degree, and on his arrival in France Charles sent ambassadors to various European countries endeavouring, with mixed success, to raise funds.

*

Dr John Earle was another of the numerous English exiles in the area. When Charles was around eleven, he had been appointed as one of his tutors and also chaplain for the then Prince of Wales but had lost these and other positions when war broke out, finally being forced to flee after Charles' defeat at Worcester. He was delighted to hear that the young king had managed to get away with his life intact, and on finding out about his arrival before Charles moved out of the inn, he hurried over there to greet him. But either his memory or his eyesight were not what they used to be, because he grabbed the first servant he could find to enquire after the whereabouts of the English king, only to find that it was Charles himself whom he had accosted. There was a convivial exchange of greetings.

*

Anne Marie Louise d'Orléans, the Duchess of Montpensier, was one of those who had consoled her exiled aunt Henrietta Maria when news of her son's defeat at the Battle of Worcester had reached France; she had known the young man well, and in fact a marriage between them had been mooted but had come to nothing. Henrietta Maria had told her 'The king, my son, is incorrigible! He loves you more than ever. I have scolded him for it.' But then, Charles 'loved' a lot of women… For a time, the Queen Mother had no more idea than anyone else as to whether Charles were alive or dead, so when news reached her that he was on his way to where she was based – the Louvre in Paris – Mlle Montpensier, though not feeling well, rushed to be with Henrietta Maria to witness the return of the son in whom so many hopes for the future of England rested.

Before he made his appearance, the mother warned Mlle Montpensier, 'You will find my son looking very ridiculous, for, to save himself, he was compelled to cut off his hair, and to assume a disguise of a very extraordinary kind.'

Right on cue, Charles appeared. 'I really thought he had a very fine figure', Mlle Montpensier later recorded, 'and was looking much better than before his departure, although he had little hair, and a great deal of beard...' She listened to his tale of narrow escapes and hardships, and his 'miserable life' in Scotland before that, 'where there was not a woman to be seen', and where men thought it a sin to play the violin.

Perhaps surprisingly, Mlle Montpensier found him 'a rather bashful and timid lover, who dared not tell me all he felt'. She now spent a lot of time with Charles, and it wasn't long before he 'put on all the airs and graces which lovers are said to assume'. He 'showed great deference to my opinion', and 'stared at me without ceasing'. Eventually, Henrietta Maria raised the subject of marriage again. She did not wish to approach her father until she knew what Mlle Montpensier's own feelings on the subject were. 'I replied that I was so happy in my present position that I never thought of marrying; that I was content with the rank and wealth I possessed; that I had everything I wished...' She did, nevertheless ask for time to think about it. Henrietta Maria agreed to this, and assured her that she would 'still be mistress of her own wealth' even when married to Charles. She would be 'the happiest person in the world' from the tenderness the king her son would have for her. Anne Marie was aware, though, that her father wasn't happy with the idea of her marrying Charles, and she herself was troubled at the idea of marrying someone in such circumstances as the homeless king of England found himself.

Charles approached her again, saying he wanted nothing more than to reclaim his kingdom and take her there as his wife – to which Anne Marie replied that it would be hard for him to do that unless he went back to England to fight for it.

'What – as soon as I have married you, do you desire that I should leave you?' Charles exclaimed.

'Yes,' came the uncompromising reply. He was 'not worthy to wear a crown if unwilling to seek it at the point of a sword' rather than spending his time in Paris dancing and amusing himself.

However much he loved Anna Marie, it must have been hard for Charles, who had only recently seen men slaughtered around him in their hundreds and who had escaped with his own life by the skin of his teeth, not to react to this almost callously flippant (and for a king who had no army to lead, rather naïve) statement. In fact, Charles remained on good terms with her, but Anne Marie began to worry that, having decided that she couldn't marry him, his attentions might discourage other princes from courting her. 'Therefore,' she decided, 'the sooner the affair was broken off the better'.

*

Charles had been through more than many people could bear during his childhood and into his early adulthood. The disintegration of his kingdom, the execution of his father, the moving from place to place as the enemy closed in on him, the attempted return ending disastrously at Worcester – all of which culminated in him abruptly finding himself leading an artificial kind of existence after having spent so much time in the 'real' world with 'real' people, a king without a kingdom (a point which Mlle Montpensier had made to him quite bluntly). And it perhaps got to him more than people realised. Sir Richard Browne, who had been a sheriff of London before being arrested in 1648, was in Paris during the time Charles was in exile there and noticed that 'for the most part that cheerfulness which against his nature he strove to shew at his first coming hither lasted but a few days, and he is very silent always, whether he be with his mother or in any company'.

Commentary:

- Allan Fea (*The Flight of the King*) refers to one of the merchants in Rouen who helped Charles as 'James Samburne', but a Samborne/Sanborn family history published in 1899 (see Bibliography) draws attention to one of the numerous petitions submitted by those who aided Charles, including one from two brothers: Thomas and John Samborne, (who had had to flee Britain because of their Royalist disposition) hoping that His Majesty might appoint one of them the post of Commissioner of the Excise Office in recognition of their 'great services' in helping not only the king but various 'persons of quality' in exile. Samborne retained certain items of Charles' old disguise as 'a relic of honour'. As the time approached when Charles was expected to return to claim his throne, the brothers, according to their petition, secretly ferried messages back and forth across the Channel 'when none else would sail'.

- Charles compensated for his short, inexpertly cut hair by adopting the French fashion of wig-wearing. When he eventually returned to England, the wearing of 'periwigs' or 'perukes' quickly became the standard look for men of a certain class.
- After Charles had made his triumphant return to England as king, Mlle Montpensier regretted spurning the opportunity to marry him. Pride, however, prevented her from trying to find out whether a match might still be made. She never married.

Chapter 19

Paving the Way

General George Monck was a Devonian, and a very experienced and distinguished solider. He joined the army to avoid being charged over the murder of an under-sheriff who was pursuing his father for debt (he and his brothers beat the man to the ground, then George ran him through with his sword). Later serving with distinction in the Dutch forces, he resigned and returned to England after a heated disagreement with the civil authorities. When the Irish regiment he had charge of was sent to England at the outbreak of the civil war, he and his fellow officers were expected to swear their allegiance to King Charles I, but Monck refused and was imprisoned till being released by Charles himself. For a man with a reputation for obstinacy and a short temper, Monck was to prove a surprisingly good diplomat and strategist in the years to come. And in a way, his refusal to swear allegiance to the king was an early sign of this.

He was captured by Parliamentarians during the siege of Nantwich in 1644, and imprisoned. Support in high places ensured his release towards the end of 1646, when he agreed to swear to fight for Parliament – there is an unsubstantiated rumour that before his release he told a fellow prisoner he intended to support Charles II's cause.

Monck's service in Ireland earned him promotion and command of the Commonwealth forces there. Things ended badly, however, when it emerged that he had been trying to arrange an unauthorized armistice with the Irish rebels. He avoided prison this time but lost his command. Once things had blown over, he returned to the army, and in fact fought alongside Oliver Cromwell when he found himself campaigning in Scotland again. Monck's talent was clear, and his star was rising once more. Promotion followed, but he fell ill at the same time that Charles was starting out on his epic journey south in disguise and he was obliged to leave the army to recover his health.

He was soon back in action, however – first at sea when war broke out with the Dutch, then on land to quell an uprising in Scotland, where Cromwell appointed him commander-in-chief. He was successful in restoring peace and remained there for several years.

Charles approached Monck from exile in 1655, but whatever the latter's feelings were at that time concerning a restoration of the monarchy, his loyalty to Cromwell came first and he immediately informed his commander-in-chief of Charles' letter. Despite rumours that Monck was the man with the military clout to pave the way for Charles' return, and whatever his deeper feelings might be telling him, for now Monck played the game with a straight bat. But these were politically turbulent times and Monck, secure in his Scottish stronghold watched, and waited.

Charles' nemesis Oliver Cromwell died in 1658, seven years after the king had fled his kingdom. In fact, Cromwell departed this life on 3 September, the anniversary of the victory at Worcester that had set Charles' flight into motion. His son Richard assumed the title of Lord Protector and Monck initially supported him. But Richard was in an invidious position. He wasn't a military man like his father, so didn't inspire the loyalty of the army; Parliament was divided between regicides, discontented Presbyterians and Royalists, and the country was heavily in debt. Richard had neither the force of personality nor the authority to enable him to impose himself on the situation, and ultimately lacked the support of the army. He lasted only nine months before withdrawing from public life. Ironically, he eventually followed Charles' lead, seeking refuge in France in the same year that Charles made the return journey (albeit Charles made the journey via Holland).

After Oliver Cromwell's death, Monck was again contacted by Charles through intermediaries; his position under the new regime wasn't as strong as it had been before, but still he bided his time in Scotland, where he was militarily secure and under no pressure to move precipitously. But amid the in-fighting south of the border, there were those in England who increasingly saw him as the strong man who could ensure a smooth passage for Charles to return; before the end of 1659 he accepted an appointment as commander-in-chief of Parliament's forces, and early in the New Year he made his move. Any semblance of opposition melted away before him as he marched south, and he was able to enter London without any blood having been spilt.

On his journey he had come to see how unpopular the Rump Parliament was in the country and he arrived in London to find it at odds with Parliament itself. He was ordered to assert his authority on the Royalist-leaning City. But Monck insisted that Parliament, which had excluded

Presbyterian members who supported Charles, dissolve itself and that new elections take place for a Convention Parliament – one which didn't pledge itself to either the Commonwealth or the monarchy. Monck himself stood and was elected to this Parliament. It was on his advice that Charles moved from Brussels to the Dutch port of Breda, the implication of which was obvious.

George Monck had the army, and, in effect (as far as his ultimate goal went) the country behind him. He was the man who would pave the way for the return of the king.

Chapter 20

The Return of the King

As seen through the eyes of Samuel Pepys

1 January 1660

The condition of the State was thus; viz. the Rump, after being disturbed by my Lord Lambert, was lately returned to sit again. The officers of the Army all forced to yield. Lawson lies still in the river, and Monk is with his army in Scotland. Only my Lord Lambert is not yet come into the Parliament, nor is it expected that he will without being forced to it.

> The original Rump had been forcibly dissolved in April 1653 when Cromwell, angry that MPs had ignored an agreement to suspend Parliament in order to prepare for elections, descended upon it at the head of a group of musketeers and ejected all members present. There followed a purge of senior army officers, many of whom had outlived their usefulness.

The new Common Council of the City do speak very high; and had sent to Monk their sword-bearer, to acquaint him with their desires for a free and full Parliament, which is at present the desires, and the hopes, and expectation of all. Twenty-two of the old secluded members having been at the House-door the last week to demand entrance, but it was denied them; and it is believed that they nor the people will be satisfied till the House be filled.

> The Common Council of the City, also known as the Court of Common Council, consisted of the mayor, aldermen and 'commonor' council men.

4 January 1660

I…went and walked in the Hall, where I heard that the Parliament spent this day in fasting and prayer; and in the afternoon came letters from the North, that brought certain news that my Lord Lambert his forces were all forsaking him, and that he was left with only fifty horse, and that he did now declare for the Parliament himself; and that my Lord Fairfax did also rest satisfied, and had laid down his arms, and that what he had done was only to secure the country against my Lord Lambert his raising of money, and free quarter.

> When Pepys' referred to the 'Hall' he meant Westminster Hall. 'My Lord Fairfax' was Sir Thomas ('Black Tom' on account of his dark hair and complexion) Fairfax, commander-in-chief of the Parliamentary army during the civil war.

9 January 1660

Thence I went with Muddiman to the Coffee-House, and gave 18d to be entered of the Club. Thence into the Hall, where I heard for certain that Monk was coming to London, and that Bradshaw's lodgings were preparing for him.

> Henry Muddiman was a journalist friend, a prominent writer on government newspapers. John Bradshaw was the judge who presided over the trial of Charles I. He had died the previous year and Pepys is referring to the use of his old rooms.
>
> Coffee houses (and coffee itself) were a recent phenomenon but had quickly sprung up in large numbers and became an essential part of everyday life for people like Pepys. They were places where people met to pick up the latest political news and gossip. The authorities were nervous about this development because of the way coffee houses became centres for 'seditious' discussion and movements.

18 January 1660

All the world is at a loss to think what Monk will do: the City saying that he will be for them, and the Parliament saying he will be for them.

21 January 1660

Then back again to Steadman's at the Mitre, in Fleet-street, in our way calling on Mr Fage, who told me how the City have some hopes of Monk.

> The Mitre was a favourite haunt of Ben Johnson's, and Steadman was the landlord at this time. It was destroyed in the Great Fire.

3 Feb 1660

After dinner I left them and went to hear news, but only found that the Parliament House was most of them with Monk at White Hall, and that in his passing through the town he had many calls to him for a free Parliament... The town and guards are already full of Monk's soldiers.

6 Feb 1660

So back to Westminster...where we found the soldiers all set in the Palace Yard, to make way for General Monk to come to the House. At the Hall we parted, and meeting Swan, he and I to the Swan and drank our morning draft. So back again to the Hall, where I stood upon the steps and saw Monk go by, he making observance to the judges as he went along.

11 Feb 1660

He told us that they [Parliament] had sent Scott and Robinson to him [Monk] this afternoon, but he would not hear them. And that the Mayor and Aldermen had offered him their own houses for himself and his officers; and that his soldiers would lack for nothing. And indeed I saw many people give the soldiers drink and money, and all along in the streets cried, 'God bless them!' and extraordinary good words. Hence we went to a merchant's house hard by, where Lock wrote a note and left, where I saw Sir Nich. Crisp, and so we went to the Star Tavern (Monk being then at Benson's), where we dined and I wrote a letter to my Lord from thence. In Cheapside there was a great many bonfires, and Bow bells and all the bells in all the churches as we went home were a-ringing. Hence we went homewards, it being about ten o'clock. But the common joy that was every where to be seen! The number of bonfires, there being fourteen between St. Dunstan's and Temple Bar, and at Strand Bridge I could at one view tell thirty-one fires…

> Thomas Scott was one of the Regicides, and he was executed after the Restoration. He and Luke Robinson had been sent as Parliamentary emissaries to see Monck before he had entered London but are suspected to have been acting more in the role of spies, trying to gauge Monck's mood and intentions, rather than diplomats.
> Sir Nicholas Crisp was a Royalist merchant.
> The Star was down an alley off Cheapside. 'Benson's', also on Cheapside, was actually The Bull's Head and Pepys is referring to it by the name of a previous landlord.

17 Feb 1660

Hence we went to White Hall, thinking to hear more news, where I met with Mr Hunt, who told me how Monk had sent for all his goods that he had here into the City; and yet again he told me, that some of the members of the House had this day laid in firing into their lodgings at White Hall for a good while, so that we are at a great stand to think what will become of things, whether Monk will stand to the Parliament or no.

> John Hunt had been a neighbour of Pepys.

20 Feb 1660

I went forth to Westminster Hall, where I met with Chetwind, Simons, and Gregory. And with them to Marsh's at Whitehall to drink, and staid there a pretty while reading a pamphlet well writ and directed to General Monk, in praise of the form of monarchy which was settled here before the wars.

> Chetwind and Simons were former work colleagues of Pepys'.
> Marsh's was a tavern.

21 Feb 1660

In the morning going out I saw many soldiers going towards Westminster, and was told that they were going to admit the secluded members again. So I to Westminster Hall, and in Chancery Row I saw about twenty of them who had been at White Hall with General Monk, who came thither this morning, and made a speech to them, and recommended to them a Commonwealth, and against Charles Stuart. They came to the House and went in one after another, and at last the Speaker came... Mr Prin came with an old basket-hilt sword on, and had a great many great shouts upon his going into the Hall. They sat till noon, and at their coming out Mr Crew saw me, and bid me come to his house, which I did, and he would have me dine with him, which I did; and he very joyful told me that the House had made General Monk, General of all the Forces in England, Scotland, and Ireland... .

> The 'secluded members' were those MPs (mostly Presbyterian) who didn't support the New Model Army, expelled from Parliament during 'Pride's Purge' in 1648.
>
> Monck's speech 'against Charles Stuart' wasn't so much anti-Royalist as anti-public disorder. He urged members to keep away from Charles and his adherents and called for the suppression of 'all tumults, stirrings and unlawful assemblies'.
>
> William Prynne, MP for Bath, was a leading Puritan. Although one of the secluded members, he had managed to sneak into a session of Parliament the previous year, causing it to be adjourned, and made other unsuccessful attempts.

3 Mar 1660

Great also is the dispute now in the House, in whose name the writs shall run for the next Parliament; and it is said that Mr Prin, in open House, said, "In King Charles's."

5 Mar 1660

Then we parted, and so to Westminster by water, only seeing Mr Pinkney at his own house, where he shewed me how he had kept the Lion and Unicorn, in the back of his chimney, bright, in expectation of the King's coming again. At home I found Mr Hunt, who told me how the Parliament had voted that the Covenant be printed and hung in churches again.

Great hopes of the King's coming again.

To bed.

> The Covenent is explained earlier. Although it was a Scottish innovation, it was accepted by the English Parliament (as it was by Charles himself) in return for Scottish military support for the Parliamentarian cause. However, senior army officers against the Covenant eventually prevented its adoption in England.

6 Mar 1660

I called Mr Sheply and we both went up to my Lord's lodgings at Mr Crew's, where he bade us to go home again, and get a fire against an hour after. Which we did at White Hall, whither he came, and after talking with him and me about his going to sea, he called me by myself to go along with him into the garden, where he asked me how things were with me...and he would use all his own, and all the interest of his friends that he had in England, to do me good. And asked me whether I could, without too much inconvenience, go to sea as his secretary, and bid me think of it. He also began to talk of things of State, and told me that he should want one in that capacity at sea, that he might trust in, and therefore he would have me to go.

He told me also, that he did believe the King would come in, and did discourse with me about it, and about the affection of the people and City, at which I was full glad... My Lord told me, that there was great endeavours to bring in the Protector again; but he told me, too, that he did believe it would not last long if he were brought in; no, nor the King neither (though he seems to think that he will come in), unless he carry himself very soberly and well. Every body now drinks the King's health without any fear, whereas before it was very private that a man dare do it. Monk this day is feasted at Mercers' Hall, and is invited one after another to all the twelve Halls in London! Many think that he is honest yet, and some or more think him to be a fool that would raise himself, but think that he will undo himself by endeavouring it.

> John Crew was Presbyterian who had been one of the secluded members. He was in a position to help Pepys because he had been one of the group sent out to invite Charles back to England, and became a Councilor of State when he was re-admitted to Parliament this month.
>
> When Pepys writes of 'my Lord' he is referring to the Earl of Sandwich, Sir Edward Mountagu, a Cromwellian who had served in his navy – yet was not a staunch republican and changed sides just before the Restoration.
>
> The 'Protector' Pepys refers to is Richard Cromwell, who was in exile, was never summoned to return, and almost certainly didn't want to be.
>
> Mercers' Hall was the home of the Worshipful Company of Mercers, one of the Great Twelve London livery companies: ancient and powerful trade associations.

10 Mar 1660

Then by coach home, where I took occasion to tell my wife of my going to sea, who was much troubled at it…

16 Mar 1660

To-night I am told, that yesterday, about five o'clock in the afternoon, one came with a ladder to the Great Exchange, and wiped with a brush the inscription that was upon King Charles, and that there was a great bonfire made in the Exchange, and people called out "God bless King Charles the Second!" From the Hall I went home to bed, very sad in mind to part with my wife, but God's will be done.

23 Mar 1660

My Lord and the Captain in one, and W. Howe and I, &c., in the other, to the Long Reach, where the Swiftsure lay at anchor… Soon as my Lord on board, the guns went off bravely from the ships… I to the cabin allotted for me, which was the best that any had that belonged to my Lord.

> The *Swiftsure* was one of the leading English warships of the day.

24 Mar 1660

The boy Eliezer flung down a can of beer upon my papers which made me give him a box of the ear, it having all spoiled my papers and cost me a great deal of work. So to bed.

1 April 1660

This day Captain Guy come on board from Dunkirk, who tells me that the King will come in, and that the soldiers at Dunkirk do drink the King's health in the streets.

8 April 1660

(Lord's day). Very calm again, and I pretty well, but my head aked all day. About noon set sail; in our way I see many vessels and masts, which are now the greatest guides for ships. We had a brave wind all the afternoon, and overtook two good merchantmen that overtook us yesterday, going to the East Indies.

21 April 1660

This day dined Sir John Boys and some other gentlemen formerly great Cavaliers, and among the rest one Mr Norwood, for whom my Lord give a convoy to carry him to the Brill, but he is certainly going to the King. For my Lord commanded me that I should not enter his name in my book… All their discourse and others are of the King's coming, and we begin to speak of it very freely. And heard how in many churches in London, and upon many signs there, and upon merchants' ships in the river, they had set up the King's arms.

Henry Norwood was a Royalist colonel in the civil war and subsequently active in trying to pave the way for Charles' return.

27 April 1660

After dinner in the afternoon came on board Sir Thomas Hatton and Sir R. Maleverer going for Flushing; but all the world know that they go where the rest of the many gentlemen go that every day flock to the King at Breda.

Hatton and Maleverer were two Royalist politicians.

1 May 1660

To-day I hear they were very merry at Deal, setting up the King's flag upon one of their maypoles, and drinking his health upon their knees in the streets, and firing the guns, which the soldiers of the Castle threatened; but durst not oppose.

2 May 1660

Great joy all yesterday at London, and at night more bonfires than ever, and ringing of bells, and drinking of the King's health upon their knees in the streets, which methinks is a little too much. But every body seems to be very joyfull in the business, insomuch that our sea-commanders now begin to say so too, which a week ago they would not do. And our seamen, as many as had money or credit for drink, did do nothing else this evening.

3 May 1660

This morning my Lord showed me the King's declaration and his letter to the two Generals to be communicated to the fleet. The contents of the letter are his offer of grace to all that will come in within forty days, only excepting them that the Parliament shall hereafter except... The letter dated at Breda, April, 4 1660, in the 12th year of his reign. Upon the receipt of it this morning by an express, Mr Phillips, one of the messengers of the Council from General Monk, my Lord summoned a council of war… Which done, the Commanders all came on board, and the council sat in the coach (the first council of war that had been in my time), where I read the letter and declaration; and while they were discoursing upon it, I seemed to draw up a vote, which being offered, they passed. Not one man seemed to say no to it, though I am confident many in their hearts were against it. After this was done, I went up to the quarter-deck with my Lord and the Commanders, and there read both the papers and the vote; which done, and demanding their opinion, the seamen did all of them cry out, 'God bless King Charles!' with the greatest joy imaginable.

> The declaration Pepys speaks of became known as the Declaration of Breda, in which Charles sympathises with 'the great many troubles and miseries which the whole Nation hath groaned under', giving thanks that a fleet has put out to sea to bring him home, and assuring his 'gracious purpose' towards all in the army and navy.

5 May 1660

This evening came Dr Clarges to Deal, going to the King; where the towns-people strewed the streets with herbes against his coming, for joy of his going. Never was there so general a content as there is now. I cannot but remember that our parson did, in his prayer to-night, pray for the long life and happiness of our King and dread Soveraign, that may last as long as the sun and moon endureth.

> Thomas Clarges was Monck's brother-in-law and sent by him to assure Charles of the army's support for him.

11 May 1660

Up very early in the morning, and so about a great deal of business in order to our going hence to-day... This morning we began to pull down all the State's arms in the fleet, having first sent to Dover for painters and others to come to set up the King's.

13 May 1660

Then to the quarter-deck, upon which the tailors and painters were at work, cutting out some pieces of yellow cloth into the fashion of a crown and C. R. and put it upon a fine sheet, and that into the flag instead of the State's arms... .

14 May 1660

In the morning when I woke and rose, I saw myself out of the scuttle close by the shore, which afterwards I was told to be the Dutch shore; the Hague was clearly to be seen by us.

17 May 1660

Before dinner Mr Edw. Pickering and I, W. Howe, Pim, and my boy, to Scheveling, where we took coach, and so to the Hague, where walking, intending to find one that might show us the King incognito, I met with Captain Whittington...and he did promise me to do it... At dinner in came Dr Cade, a merry mad parson of the King's. And they two after dinner got the child and me (the others not being able to crowd in) to see the King, who kissed the child very affectionately. Then we kissed his, and the Duke of York's, and the Princess Royal's hands. The King seems to be a very sober man; and a very splendid Court he hath in the number of persons of quality that are about him, English very rich in habit.

> The Duke of York was Charles' brother James, and the Princess Royal (the first to go by that title) was his sister Mary, the widow of William II, Prince of Orange and mother of the future William III of England.

23 May 1660

In the morning came infinity of people on board from the King to go along with him.

My Lord, Mr Crew, and others, go on shore to meet the King as he comes off from shore, where Sir R. Stayner bringing His Majesty into the boat, I hear that His Majesty did with a great deal of affection kiss my Lord upon his first meeting.

The King, with the two Dukes and Queen of Bohemia, Princess Royal, and Prince of Orange, came on board, where I in their coming in kissed the King's, Queen's, and Princess's hands, having done the other before. Infinite shooting off of the guns, and that in a disorder on purpose, which was better than if it had been otherwise.

All day nothing but Lords and persons of honour on board, that we were exceeding full… .

After dinner the King and Duke altered the name of some of the ships, viz. the Nazeby into Charles; the Richard, James… That done, the Queen, Princess Royal, and Prince of Orange, took leave of the King, and the Duke of York went on board the London, and the Duke of Gloucester, the Swiftsure. Which done, we weighed anchor, and with a fresh gale and most happy weather we set sail for England. All the afternoon the King walked here and there, up and down (quite contrary to what I thought him to have been), very active and stirring.

Upon the quarterdeck he fell into discourse of his escape from Worcester, where it made me ready to weep to hear the stories that he told of his difficulties that he had passed through, as his travelling four days and three nights on foot, every step up to his knees in dirt, with nothing but a green coat and a pair of country breeches on, and a pair of country shoes that made him so sore all over his feet, that he could scarce stir. Yet he was forced to run away from a miller and other company, that took them for rogues.

His sitting at table at one place, where the master of the house, that had not seen him in eight years, did know him, but kept it private; when at the same table there was one that had been of his own regiment at Worcester, could not know him, but made him drink the King's health, and said that the King was at least four fingers higher than he.

At another place he was by some servants of the house made to drink, that they might know him not to be a Roundhead, which they swore he was.

In another place at his inn, the master of the house, as the King was standing with his hands upon the back of a chair by the fire-side, kneeled down and kissed his hand, privately, saying, that he would not ask him who he was, but bid God bless him whither he was going. Then the difficulty of getting a boat to get into France, where he was fain to plot with the master thereof to keep his design from the four men and a boy (which was all his ship's company), and so got to Fecamp in France.

At Rouen he looked so poorly, that the people went into the rooms before he went away to see whether he had not stole something or other... .

So to my cabin again, where the company still was, and were talking more of the King's difficulties; as how he was fain to eat a piece of bread and cheese out of a poor boy's pocket; how, at a Catholique house, he was fain to lie in the priest's hole a good while in the house for his privacy.

After that our company broke up, and the Doctor and I to bed. We have all the Lords Commissioners on board us, and many others. Under sail all night, and most glorious weather.

> Charles was always ready to tell the tell of his escape to France, something that perhaps helped to fix it in his mind well enough for him to recount it in detail to Pepys nearly twenty years from this date, to be recorded for posterity.

25 May 1660

By the morning we were come close to the land, and every body made ready to get on shore.

The King and the two Dukes did eat their breakfast before they went, and there being set some ship's diet before them, only to show them the manner of the ship's diet, they eat of nothing else but pease and pork, and boiled beef... .

I went, and Mr Mansell, and one of the King's footmen, with a dog that the King loved, (which shit in the boat, which made us laugh, and me think that a King and all that belong to him are but just as others are), in a boat by ourselves, and so got on shore when the King did, who was received by General Monk with all imaginable love and respect at his entrance upon the land of Dover. Infinite the crowd of people and the horsemen, citizens, and noblemen of all sorts.

The Mayor of the town came and gave him his white staff, the badge of his place, which the King did give him again. The Mayor also presented him from the town a very rich Bible, which he took and said it was the thing that he loved above all things in the world.

A canopy was provided for him to stand under, which he did, and talked awhile with General Monk and others, and so into a stately coach there set for him, and so away through the town towards Canterbury, without making any stay at Dover. The shouting and joy expressed by all is past imagination…. .

21 April 1661

(Lord's day). In the morning we were troubled to hear it rain as it did, because of the great show tomorrow. After I was ready I walked to my father's... Here dined Doctor Thos. Pepys and Dr Fayrebrother; and all our talk about to-morrow's show, and our trouble that it is like to be a wet day… Then I went home, and all the way is so thronged with people to see the triumphal arches, that I could hardly pass for them.

> Thomas Pepys was Samuel's cousin. Fayrebrother (Fairbrother) probably accompanied him to London, as they both seem to have been Cambridge men.

22 April 1661

King's going from ye Tower to Whitehall.

Up early and made myself as fine as I could, and put on my velvet coat, the first day that I put it on, though made half a year ago... Went to Mr Young's, the flag-maker, in Corne-hill; and there we had a good room to ourselves, with wine and good cake, and saw the show very well. In which it is impossible to relate the glory of this day, expressed in the clothes of them that rid, and their horses and horses clothes... The Knights of the Bath was a brave sight of itself; and their Esquires, among which Mr Armiger was an Esquire to one of the Knights. Remarquable were the two men that represent the two Dukes of Normandy and Aquitane.

The Bishops come next after Barons… My Lord Monk rode bare after the King, and led in his hand a spare horse, as being Master of the Horse. The King, in a most rich embroidered suit and cloak, looked most noble… .

The streets all gravelled, and the houses hung with carpets before them, made brave show… So glorious was the show with gold and silver, that we were not able to look at it, our eyes at last being so much overcome with it. Both the King and the Duke of York took notice of us, as he saw us at the window.

> William Armiger was a 'cousin' (actually rather more distantly
> related than that) of Pepys who lodged with his brother Tom.

23 April 1661

About 4 I rose and got to the Abbey…and with much ado, by the favour of Mr Cooper, his man, did get up into a great scaffold across the North end of the Abbey, where with a great deal of patience I sat from past 4 till 11 before the King came in. And a great pleasure it was to see the Abbey raised in the middle, all covered with red, and a throne (that is a chair) and footstool on the top of it; and all the officers of all kinds, so much as the very fidlers [sic], in red vests.

At last comes in the Dean and Prebends of Westminster, with the Bishops (many of them in cloth of gold copes), and after them the Nobility, all in their Parliament robes, which was a most magnificent sight. Then the Duke, and the King with a scepter (carried by my Lord Sandwich) and sword and mond before him, and the crown too.

The King in his robes, bare-headed, which was very fine. And after all had placed themselves, there was a sermon and the service; and then in the Quire at the high altar, the King passed through all the ceremonies of the Coronacon, which to my great grief I and most in the Abbey could not see. The crown being put upon his head, a great shout begun, and he came forth to the throne, and there passed more ceremonies: as taking the oath, and having things read to him by the Bishop; and his lords (who put on their caps as soon as the King put on his crown) and bishops come, and kneeled before him.

And three times the King at Arms went to the three open places on the scaffold, and proclaimed, that if any one could show any reason why Charles Stewart should not be King of England, that now he should come and speak.

And a Generall Pardon also was read by the Lord Chancellor, and meddalls flung up and down by my Lord Cornwallis, of silver, but I could not come by any.

But so great a noise that I could make but little of the musique; and indeed, it was lost to every body. But I had so great a list to pisse that I went out a little while before the King had done all his ceremonies, and went round the Abbey to Westminster Hall, all the way within rayles, and 10,000 people, with the ground covered with blue cloth; and scaffolds all the way. Into the Hall I got, where it was very fine with hangings and scaffolds one upon another full of brave ladies; and my wife in one little one, on the right hand.

Here I staid walking up and down, and at last upon one of the side stalls I stood and saw the King come in with all the persons (but the soldiers) that were yesterday in the cavalcade; and a most pleasant sight it was to see them in their several robes. And the King came in with his crown on, and his sceptre in his hand, under a canopy borne up by six silver staves, carried by Barons of the Cinque Ports, and little bells at every end.

And after a long time, he got up to the farther end, and all set themselves down at their several tables; and that was also a brave sight: and the King's first course carried up by the Knights of the Bath. And many fine ceremonies there was of the Heralds leading up people before him, and bowing; and my Lord of Albemarle's going to the kitchin and eat a bit of the first dish that was to go to the King's table.

But, above all, was these three Lords, Northumberland, and Suffolk, and the Duke of Ormond, coming before the courses on horseback, and staying so all dinner-time, and at last to bring up the King's Champion [Dymock], all in armour on horseback, with his spear and targett carried before him. And a Herald proclaims 'That if any dare deny Charles Stewart to be lawful King of England, here was a Champion that would fight with him;' and with these words, the Champion flings down his gauntlet, and all this he do three times in his going up towards the King's table. At last when he is come, the King drinks to him, and then sends him the cup which is of gold, and he drinks it off, and then rides back again with the cup in his hand... .

And strange it is to think, that these two days have held up fair till now that all is done, and the King gone out of the Hall; and then it fell a-raining and thundering and lightening as I have not seen it do for some years: which people did take great notice of; God's blessing of the work of these two days, which is a foolery to take too much notice of such things... .

Mr Hunt and I went in with Mr Thornbury (who did give the company all their wine, he being yeoman of the wine-cellar to the King) to his house; and there, with his wife and two of his sisters, and some gallant sparks that were there, we drank the King's health, and nothing else, till one of the gentlemen fell down stark drunk, and there lay spewing; and I went to my Lord's pretty well. But no sooner a-bed with Mr Shepley but my head began to hum, and I to vomit, and if ever I was foxed it was now...

Now, after all this, I can say that, besides the pleasure of the sight of these glorious things, I may now shut my eyes against any other objects, nor for the future trouble myself to see things of state and show, as being sure never to see the like again in this world.

> The day's proceedings didn't go entirely smoothly. An unseemly scuffle broke out between the Barons of the Cinque Ports who had accompanied the king holding a canopy aloft, and the king's footmen who 'most insolently and violently' tried to grab it from them once Charles had taken his place on the throne. A tug-of-war ensued, with the barons being hauled all the way to one end of the hall, grimly clinging on to their trophy. The contest was brought to an end when Charles, who had been alerted to what was happening, sent officers to arrest and dismiss from their posts his own footmen.

Chapter 21

Long to Reign Over Us

The reign of Charles II is often characterized as a hedonistic rebound against the grim constraints of puritanism, with its condemnation of Christmas celebrations, the theatre and so on and included in this, perhaps, his own over-compensation for the struggles, dangers and privations he experienced in his life before becoming king. He is portrayed as a decadent, spendthrift playboy, one whose lifestyle earned him the nickname of the Merry Monarch. Although his wife's three, possibly four pregnancies ended in stillbirths or miscarriages, Charles fathered at least twelve (the estimates go as high as seventeen) illegitimate children by up to eight women, starting two years before the battle of Worcester when he was eighteen and living in Rotterdam. As much as all this, it was the money lavished on his court and favourites, and the blatant and unashamed nature of his affairs with people women like Barbara Villiers and Nell Gwyn, which became the subject of gossip, dismay and ridicule. It's also true that Charles was renowned for becoming easily bored with the administrative side of his duties and impatient with Parliament – but he was no George IV. Compared to what the country had been going through for decades, and from a religious point of view for centuries – not just the bloodshed but the restrictions on liberties imposed by the Puritans – any half-decent monarch was probably always going to be allowed a fair amount of leeway as long as there was a degree of stability and tolerance in the country.

And Charles did have his serious side. Had a genuine interest in the arts and sciences and was a patron in these fields as well as in education. He founded the Royal Society, was a patron of Wren during his efforts to rebuild London after the Great Fire of 1666 and founded the Royal Hospital in Chelsea to provide a home for old soldiers. He also had a keen interest in the navy and naval matters – even though his perennial money problems meant that he wasn't always able to fund that institution properly – something which would eventually have a catastrophic and humiliating result.

Charles married the long-suffering Catherine of Braganza of Portugal in 1662. Like all such marriages it was more a political arrangement than a love match, but even despite Charles' persistent philandering there does seem to have been some genuine affection. When Catherine fell seriously ill in 1663, Charles (as Pepys tells us) was constantly at her bedside. She survived, and in fact went on to outlive Charles by twenty years.

So, after the often-harrowing years of religious persecution, torture and execution under Mary and Elizabeth, and to a certain extent James I, accompanied by the threat of Spanish invasion and ultimately an England at war with itself, Charles' reign was a relatively peaceful one, disturbed only by ongoing conflicts with the Dutch.

Holland was proving to be a troublesome rival to Britain's Empire-building ambitions and rivalry over territories in Africa and North America was a particularly thorny issue. The two nations had been antagonists during Charles' period of exile until the signing of a treaty, but even now there were many in Britain who had concerns that their country risked being put at an economic and military disadvantage as a result of Holland's growth unless strong action was taken; this was exacerbated by fears over Dutch links with the remnants of Britain's republican and radical groups. Charles wasn't oblivious to this but had no desire to rush into war – especially one the country's coffers might struggle to fund. But British provocation – attacking Dutch ships and overseas territories (including the capture of New Amsterdam, later to become New York) played a big part in sparking a resumption of war, which Britain declared formally in March 1665.

The conflict rumbled on inconclusively until, by the middle of 1666, money was running out in Britain, a situation not helped by plague the previous year and the Great Fire that September. A shocking and humbling consequence of Britain's financial plight came in 1667, when a Dutch squadron was able to sail unhindered up the Thames and destroy naval ships laid-up through lack of money. More embarrassingly still, under the eyes of the helpless onlookers, the Dutch calmly towed away the navy's flagship, the *Royal Charles*. Charles had little choice but to enter into another peace treaty with Holland, and the conflict was brought to an end. The peace was short-lived however. Five years later, England was once again at war with Holland, but under very different circumstances. Two years previously, England had entered into an alliance with France, but what few people knew was that there was a secret version of the treaty in which Charles agreed, among other things, to assist France in defeating the Dutch, and that Charles himself would convert to Catholicism in return for much-needed financial aid from France. There was no specific time limit set within which Charles had to convert (the wording was 'as soon as the welfare of his kingdom will permit'), and the secret treaty never came to light in his lifetime, but when France attacked Holland in 1672, England was obliged to support Louis XIV. Although this became known as the 'Disaster Year' in Holland, the Dutch managed to hold out against complete conquest, and once again the conflict ended in a negotiated settlement.

A later crisis in Charles' reign came courtesy of a shady character called Titus Oates and what became known as the Popish Plot, of 1678. Oates became an Anglican priest on the strength of lying about having graduated at Cambridge (he actually dropped out); a secret homosexual himself, he falsely accused a schoolmaster of the same sin, as it was then, in an effort to get his job. (It backfired and he was charged with perjury but fled before his trial.) He joined the navy as a chaplain and was thrown out for sodomy, then made an opportunistic conversion to Catholicism and joined a Spanish Jesuit college, from which he was soon expelled. This, then, is the man whose outlandish tales of a Catholic plot to kill Charles, despite its flaws and contradictions and the scepticism of numerous senior statesmen, snowballed into a kind of hysterical paranoia and threw the country (or at least London) into turmoil. Charles himself was far too sharp for Oates and easily saw through his obfuscations, but his Parliament took the idea of the plot very seriously. Catholics were banished from London, many Jesuits were put to death and the witch hunt nearly destroyed the lives of innocent men including Samuel Pepys, who was falsely implicated and spent a couple of months in the Tower before his name was cleared.

One aspect of the Popish Plot was the idea that Charles would be done away with in order to allow his Catholic brother James, Duke of York to take his place, which in turn served to highlight the duke's Catholicism. Charles' reign may have been more tolerant than some previous ones, but the country wasn't ready for that level of toleration; a Catholic king and possibly even attendant implications for the state religion wouldn't be countenanced. This was one of the factors that led to James' daughter Mary being married off to the Protestant William of Orange – a move which would have future repercussions for the house of Stuart when in 1688 James II, having succeeded Charles, became the latest of his line to be forced into exile, this time in favour of William and Mary.

Political and religious toleration were a feature of Charles' reign, perhaps partly arising out of a sense of pragmatism, considering how divided the country had previously been, but also, it's probably fair to say, because it was in his nature to handle people and situations in that manner. It might even be said that in trying to avoid siding too strongly with anyone, he kept everyone, including a divided Parliament, happy to some degree and thus steered a course away from further crises. He is generally viewed as a popular king, despite his run-ins with Parliament and widely criticised indulgent lifestyle.

We have seen that Charles was generous to those who helped him in his time of need. He was also quite realistic and magnanimous in his treatment of Cromwell's leading supporters and the principal members of the Commonwealth. This leniency did not apply, though, to those who had been directly responsible for the death of his father, the 'Regicides'. The list of regicides did not include only the commissioners who had signed the death warrant, but also those who sat in on the process but were not signatories.

It was too late to punish Cromwell, who had died two years before the Restoration, though his corpse was disinterred from its resting place in Westminster Abbey and hanged at Tyburn along with the bodies of other deceased regicides. Finally, Cromwell's head was cut off and impaled on a spike outside Westminster Hall. A manhunt was set in motion to apprehend the 39 still-living regicides. Some were easily caught and those who had fled abroad were pursued. John Lisle escaped to Switzerland but was cornered and assassinated by a Royalist agent, others were dealt with through more conventional diplomatic channels and extradited to stand trial in England. It was not a completely draconian or barbaric process. Not all those caught were executed (and not all *were* caught); some were imprisoned, while some of those originally sentenced to death were reprieved.

Although Charles was generous with the rewards he handed out to those who helped him, the officials at the Exchequer were not always quite so benevolent, and there are many stories of people going unpaid for long periods. A memo from 1685 listing those waiting for payment, and the amounts, shows that Jane Lane was owed £750, and brother John hadn't been paid in over five years and was £2750 down. Thankfully, the far less well-off Penderels don't appear on the list (Charles almost certainly wouldn't have countenanced them not being looked after) whose total of outstanding amounts stood at £8,732.

Not all those who petitioned the king were genuine. As soon as word spread that those who held given Charles a helping hand along the way were not only applying for financial reward but being successful, applications poured in. One such was from Mary Gibson of the Talbot Inn, Ripley, Surrey. She applied for a reward for her father's services in hiding Charles from 'a house full of soldiers', an optimistic claim bearing in mind that her hostelry was at least fifty miles from any place visited by Charles on his journey south. Even more brazen was the letter from Hanah Wyatt of Colchester, over a hundred miles north and east of his final destination of Brighton (which he approached from the west), who claimed to have given His Majesty a drink to quench his thirst as he passed her parents' house on foot. (To be fair, since the king was in disguise and there were others fleeing Worcester in a similar manner, it is possible that mistaken identity was to blame in some cases rather than downright opportunism.)

A similar phenomenon occurred when it came to places that, over the years after the Restoration, claimed to be locations which had provided Charles with shelter. These ranged as far and wide as Ipswich, Glamorgan, Cheshire and Lancashire. A story persisted at least into the twentieth century that at Coaxden Manor, Devon, the six-foot-two Charles had hidden from soldiers under the hooped skirts of Mrs Coga, the owner; another had it that he played the part of a scullery boy at a house in Carmarthenshire.

Perhaps Charles' finest hour was when he personally pitched in to help during the Great Fire of London of 1666. Where the Lord Mayor had initially contemptuously declared that 'a woman could piss it out' on being taken to the scene of the fire, and had then cried ('like a fainting woman' according to Pepys) that he didn't know what to do, Charles (along with his brother the Duke of York) after being warned by Samuel Pepys as to the extent and potentially disastrous nature of the rapidly spreading conflagration, leapt into action. He went among the Londoners to ascertain the situation, then ordered and personally supervised the pulling down of houses to create a fire break. He may have succumbed to the hedonistic lifestyle after the trials of his early life, but, almost unique among kings and queens until then and probably since, he had lived among ordinary people, shared their hardships, knew how to talk to them. He was popping up all over London, organizing, rallying and even at one point joining his brother in a human chain of people passing buckets of water to fight the fire. He is said to have been on the go for over thirty hours, finally trudging back to Westminster weary, grimy and (not for the first time in his life) with a soot-blackened face.

Knights of the Royal Oak

In the year that Charles returned to England, a proposal was made to him that a new order be created to reward those who had supported him during his exile. It was to be called the order of the Knights of the Royal Oak, a reference

147

to the tree at Boscobel in which Charles had hidden in the early stages of his escape. This wasn't just to include the few who, as described in this book, had been close to him during those desperate weeks, but extended to those who had supported him at all times before and after fleeing Britain. Neither was it to be just a select few of the London in-crowd, a phenomenon still complained of today, but a truly national selection process, with nearly 700 men from all counties of England and Wales being proposed as recipients.

It was in many ways a nice and fitting idea and a more genuine honour than most others; a recognition for tangible and important services during the monarch's darkest hours. After a little more thought, however, fears arose that in a still divided nation it might actually be a source of friction and further dissension. The recipients would, after all, inevitably be almost exclusively from among the ranks of Royalists and probably a large number of them Catholics. Another aspect of the idea was that the recipients would have had to pay for the privilege. As Antti Matikkala points out in *The Orders of Knighthood*, the proposer emphasised in his memorandum to the king that it would be 'a way of raisinge a verry Considerable Summe of money in a verry short tyme'. Bearing in mind his later financial problems, one wonders whether Charles ever regretted that the order was never instituted.

A less divisive compromise was the institution of a national day of celebration and commemoration to be held every 29 May, which was not only the day that Charles made his triumphal return to London, but also happened to be his birthday.

Oak Apple Day

The great diarist Samuel Pepys recorded in his journal dated 1 June 1660, 'that Parliament had ordered the 29th of May, the King's birthday, to be forever kept as a day of thanksgiving for our redemption from tyranny and the King's return to his Government, he returning to London that day'.

Unlike the Knights of the Royal Oak idea, this one did catch on. Although it has since died out in most parts of the country, it was celebrated for around 200 years before it was formally abolished as a national holiday by Parliament in 1859. It didn't disappear overnight, of course, and in fact is still marked in different forms and in numerous parts of England. An 'oak apple', sometimes assumed to be an acorn, is actually a roughly acorn-sized type of gall which grows from leaf buds in which wasps have inserted eggs. Oak Apple Day is known as Shick-Shack day in Hampshire, and Oak and Nettle day in other parts, including Staffordshire, where those not wearing a sprig of oak leaves in their coat or hat made themselves liable to punishment of being thrashed with nettles. In some areas, offenders might have eggs thrown at them for the same reason, in Sussex and elsewhere they could be pinched, leading to Pinch-Bum day, and Essex had its Bumping Day.

Oak Apple Day is still observed at the Chelsea Royal Hospital, founded by Charles and where his statue stands in the forecourt. A member of the royal family visits every 29 May to take part in a little ceremony there. In Worcester, a range of events take place at the Commandery, the building which served as the Royalist headquarters before the battle. Other places associated with the battle and Charles' subsequent flight also continue to mark the day, including Moseley Old Hall, where Charles took refuge.

Having been in good health, on a winter's morning in 1685 after a strangely restless night Charles woke in a distressed state, pallid and unable to speak. Before long he suffered some sort of attack, probably a stroke (possibly a second stroke, in fact, with the first having come in the night), and his doctors proceeded to subject him to a barrage of painful 'treatments' of so barbaric a nature that they would have been classed as torture had they been applied to a well person – but which treatments were considered routine or even cutting edge at the time. As well as the usual blood-letting – in great quantities in Charles' case including from the jugular vein – this regimen included being made to drink very hot urine. In spite of all this he did he did temporarily regain the power of speech, famously entreating brother James to 'let not poor Nelly starve' (referring to his long-term mistress Nell Gwyn). He even seemed to retain the calm humour in a time of crisis that had been a feature of his escape into exile over thirty years previously, apologising to those at his bedside for being 'such a time a-dying'. As we saw earlier, Father John Huddleston, who had played a significant role in keeping Charles safe after Worcester and who had helped to clothe him and tended to his shredded feet, oversaw his conversion to Catholicism. Still only 54 years old, Charles died four days after the initial attack, just before midday on 16 February.

Appendix A

Lord Henry Wilmot

Wilmot's father, Charles, was an Oxfordshire man and an Oxford graduate but also a soldier, as his son would be. Charles was posted to Ireland and was knighted in Dublin and created 1st Viscount Wilmot of Athlone in 1621 when Henry was still a boy. When Charles died in 1643 or 1644, Henry Wilmot, as the only surviving son, assumed the title when in his early thirties. He was baptised in London, and as a young man he soon followed in his father's military footsteps.

His early experience came in fighting for the Dutch against the Spanish control of their territories. Serving in the rank of captain, Wilmot was seriously wounded at the siege of Breda in 1636 – in which George Monck was also involved. After returning home and recovering, he was captured fighting for Charles I in Scotland. His captivity didn't last long, and he became the Member of Parliament for Tamworth in 1640. King Charles was at odds with Parliament by this time, and it wasn't long before Wilmot became embroiled in a plot by Charles I's followers. The plan was to bring a force stationed at York down to London to try to intimidate MPs into obedience. The scheme came to nothing, other than, from Wilmot's point of view, resulting in him being imprisoned once again – this time in the Tower of London – when the details became known to Parliament.

When civil war broke out, Wilmot was soon back in the saddle, with his own regiment of horse which saw action at Powick Bridge, Edgehill and Marlborough in the space of three months. Wilmot was wounded at Powick Bridge, the opening cavalry engagement of the civil war, but the Royalists were the victors. Edgehill ended inconclusively, but Marlborough was captured by forces led by Wilmot himself.

The following year, 1643, he followed up Marlborough with another victory just outside Devizes in Wiltshire, as part of a general Royalist strengthening of its position in the West Country. Here he defeated Major General Sir William Waller, who had previously had great success in the region, at Roundway Down. The two generals met again the following year when Wilmot also got the upper hand at the Battle of Cropredy Bridge near Banbury – despite suffering a shot to the arm and a bullet grazing his hand when leading a charge in person. By this point, Wilmot had already been created Baron Wilmot of Adderbury thanks to his achievements and had been awarded overall command of the Royalist cavalry, taking the place of the illustrious Prince Rupert.

Wilmot married twice. First to Frances Morton of Dorset, who tragically died within a year, followed by Anne Lee of Wiltshire, daughter, of Sir John St John. They seem to have only had one child – a son, John, who became the second Earl of Rochester. The Earl of Clarendon, whose writings helped fill in some of the gaps in the story of Charles' escape from Worcester, described Wilmot thus: 'He was a man proud and ambitious, and incapable of being contented; an orderly officer in marches and governing his troops. He drank hard and had a great power over all who did so, which was a great people'.

But Wilmot was humiliated in front of those troops who admired him so much in 1644, when, while he was based in Devon, news emerged that he had been engaged in secret negotiations with the Earl of Essex, then the overall commander of the Parliamentary forces, in an attempt to get Charles I to agree to peace talks. Wilmot was stripped of his command and incarcerated in Exeter. The next stage would have been a court-martial, but Wilmot's treatment caused such unrest among his men that the king overlooked this step and sent him into exile in France.

His fighting days weren't quite over even now, though. He had been engaged for some years in a dispute with his erstwhile comrade-in-arms from the Battle of Edgehill of 1642, Lord Digby, who had become an advisor to the king. (Ironically, this Digby was related to Kenelm Digby, son of the man who had tried to blow up Charles' father James in the Gunpowder Plot). Presumably feeling that the advice being given wasn't benefiting Charles, Wilmot had tried (and failed) to get Digby and another adviser dismissed. When Wilmot's attempts at brokering peace came to light, it was Digby's turn to hit back, and he pressed for strong action against Wilmot. Things came to a head in 1647 after letters critical of Wilmot, which Digby had written to the queen, had become public knowledge. In the time-honoured way, Wilmot sent a challenge to a friend of Digby via an intermediary when the latter turned up in France. Digby's nominated second in the proposed duel assured Wilmot that Digby would provide him with 'satisfaction'. But Digby must have had a habit of getting on the wrong side of people, because in the meantime he received a challenge from none other than Prince Rupert, declaring that he awaited him 'sword in hand'. News of this second challenge reached the ears of Queen Henrietta; she wasn't about to allow her son, second in line to the throne, to risk his life. She had Digby arrested. Once his differences with the prince were sorted out in a more peaceable fashion, the meeting with Wilmot was able to go ahead, at a spot just outside Paris.

The encounter was something of a farce. Digby's side insisted that the seconds should also fight 'after the French manner'. O'Neile, Wilmot's second, and Lord Wentworth for Digby, lunged at each other, collided, and fell to the ground – where the apparently rather portly Digby joined in. O'Neile reported that they 'lay grovelling till Mr Digby had like to have squeezed us to death by overbearing almost upon us as massy a bulk as himself'. The cry went up that Wilmot's sword arm had been injured. When Digby's second demanded his sword, Wilmot declared 'that they might take his life, but they would not take his sword', and Digby's side decided to leave it at that. The duel ended inconclusively and the two sides parted frostily.

But it was Wilmot's time in France that brought him into the same circles as Charles, leading to him becoming the latter's close friend and advisor. We have already seen that he accompanied Charles to Scotland and then south to what would become the Battle of Worcester and its aftermath. Soon after they made it back to France, Charles made Wilmot Earl of Rochester.

Wilmot had to escape England yet again before the Restoration. Having travelled to Marston Moor to lead a Royalist rebellion which failed before it had even started, he fled south, once again. This escape didn't go so smoothly because he was captured but then released at Aylesbury, whence he managed to rejoin Charles in France.

That Wilmot would have occupied high office for as long as he desired after the Restoration there can be no doubt, but sadly he didn't live to enjoy the fruits that his bravery and wise counsel had earned him. In working to help Charles foster an alliance between Spain and Royalists in exile, he found himself in command of a Royalist army in Bruges. But in 1658, just two years before Charles would return to England, fever spread through the encampment and claimed many lives – including that of Lord Henry Wilmot, First Earl of Rochester.

There is no questioning Wilmot's courage, and it's possible that Charles might not have succeeded in escaping his Parliamentary pursuers without him. But looking more closely at his part in the story, it's hard to avoid the conclusion that he was somewhat lucky to avoid capture, and foolhardy in not adopting some form of disguise. (Or perhaps vain, as might be read into Charles' droll criticism of him refusing because he would 'look frightfully'.) Even Charles, in his fairly elaborate disguises, encountered people who almost immediately recognised him, and on more than one occasion Wilmot's path crossed with people who knew him. Only chance dictated that those encounters were with those who wished to help rather than harm him. Nevertheless, his strategy did ultimately pay off, and it would be almost impossible to overstate his contribution to the success of Charles' flight into exile.

The Penderels

After the Restoration, the Penderel brothers were invited to London to meet Charles so that he could properly express his gratitude to them. On greeting 'Trusty Richard', who played such a big part in helping keep him safe, Charles said,

'Friend Richard, I am glad to see thee. Thou wert my preserver and conductor, the bright star that showed me to my Bethlehem, for which kindness I will engrave thy memory on the tablet of a faithful heart.'

He then addressed the assembled Lords assembled in Westminster where the reception took place:

'My lords, I pray you respect this good man for my sake.'

Turning his attention back to the perhaps blushing Richard Penderel, who was in a situation as far removed as his everyday life as could be imagined, Charles urged: 'Master Richard, be bold and tell these lords what passed amongst us when I had quitted the oak at Boscobel to reach Pit Leasow.'

Richard proceeded to briefly recount the story of how Charles had complained about the attributes of the old mill horse he had been obliged to ride, and how Humphry had pointed out that the slow pace was hardly surprising considering that the poor beast was carrying 'the weight of three kingdoms upon his back'.

The five Penderel brothers deservedly earned their place in history by providing Charles with vital support at a crucial time during his escape. His trail was still warm and the area was swarming with searchers – both local militia and members of the army which had just defeated the Royalists. The Penderels knowingly risked their own lives, ignoring the carrot of a huge reward – an amount almost beyond imagination to someone in their position – dangled in front of them. They were resourceful, ingenious, calm and courageous in their different roles.

Their surname is spelt in various ways in historical records and accounts. There is a modern 'Pendrill' Family History Society, created by descendants of the brothers with the purpose of researching their common ancestry. In referring to the brothers, I have gone with the variant most commonly used today.

The information we have on them comes in snippets appearing in the different narratives, but the vast majority of what we know is thanks to Samuel Pepys, who made a point of finding out from Father Huddleston 'what he knew touching the brotherhood of the Penderells, as to the names and qualities of each of the brothers'. Huddleston came into contact with the Penderels while working as a chaplain at Moseley Old Hall at the time when Charles made his appearance in the area.

The eldest was *William*, a tall man born around 1609, so approximately 42 when the events described in this book took place. He lived at Boscobel with his wife Joan, where he acted as caretaker. They had both been fined in the past for refusing to attend Anglican church services, at which time he was described as a yeoman. As we saw in our story, even before Charles arrived he had sheltered the Earl of Derby on his flight from the Battle of Wigan Lane – in fact it was this episode which led the latter to recommend Boscobel as a place of refuge to Charles when he met up with him at White Ladies Priory.

William and Joan looked after Charles when he was hiding in the famous oak tree (and in fact provided him with the ladder which allowed him to get into its branches). Their hospitality in the house was much appreciated by Charles and when Joan died in 1669 and was buried at White Ladies Priory, her gravestone featured a little verse describing her as 'Dame Joan', the title Charles had playfully addressed her with during his stay with them. They did pay a price for their aid, though. Rumours circulating in the neighbourhood about a possible royal visitor led to raids on Boscobel and William being taken away for questioning in in Shrewsbury. Joan is said to have been 'much affrighted' by the numerous searches of Boscobel House.

William is said to have become something of an entrepreneur once Charles had returned as king and it was safe to be open about what had happened. People were keen to see the place Charles had stayed and the tree he had hidden in, and William turned part of Boscobel House into an inn. It was one of many hostelries at that period given the name the Royal Oak, but surely the first and foremost.

He was also granted a regular pension of £100 a year. In later life his past came back to haunt him, because he became caught up in what was called the Popish Plot, which as we have seen was totally spurious story about a Catholic scheme to assassinate King Charles. However, William, his brothers and others who had helped Charles were provided with legal protection at the height of the investigations, clearly at Charles' behest even though he isn't named in the official report of the Parliamentary order:

> December 1678
> Ordered, by the Lords Spiritual and Temporal in Parliament Assembled, that Mr Charles Giffard, Francis Yates and his Wife, William Penderel, John Penderel, Richard Penderel, Humphrey Penderel, and George Penderel, Mr Thomas Whitegrave of Mosely, Collonel William Carlos, and Mr Francis Reynold of Carleson in the county of Bedford, who were Instrumental in the preservation of his Majesties Person after the battle of Worcester, or such of them as are now living shall for their said service live as freely as any of His Majesties Protestant Subjects, without being lyable or subject to the penalties of any of the Laws relating to Popish Recusants, and that a Bill be prepared and brought into this House for that purpose, and the name of Mr John Huddleston be inserted therein.

'Francis Reynold of Carleson' is actually Francis Reynolds of Carlton, who is one of the young men under the tuition of Huddleston at Moseley. He helped hold the horses of Charles' party, and may have assisted in other ways unrecorded.

William Penderel died at Boscobel in August, 1700, at the ripe old age of 91.

John Penderel lived at White Ladies and managed the woods there. He had harboured a Catholic priest, and it was because Father Huddleston had performed mass for him that John recognised him as he was walking along the lane and told him he was in need of a hiding place for Lord Wilmot.

Even though it was Richard who made the arduous journey that involved tramping for miles about the countryside in the dark guiding Charles, Father Huddleston told Pepys that it was John who 'tooke the most pains of all the brothers'.

He had been a Royalist foot soldier during the civil war and may have served under Colonel Careless at one point. John guided Wilmot on his travels in the vicinity as Richard had guided Charles, and he also ferried messages between Wilmot and the king.

Like William he was granted a £100 annuity at the Restoration as well as other smaller payments, but perhaps he wasn't as careful with his money – or was just unlucky – because it is believed that he was in debt when he died in about 1683. Later in life he was known as 'Old John of Boscobel'.

Richard was the third of the brothers. He was known as 'Trusty Richard' (or 'Trusty Dick'), apparently even before these escapades. He was a tenant farmer in a small way and a woodsman like John. A legal document issued just after the Restoration, in which he grants a friend power of attorney, shows him to have held the status of yeoman after the Restoration, which put him one rung higher up the ladder than a tenant farmer and meant he owned land of his own. It also shows that he, like George who witnessed it and almost certainly the rest of the brothers, was illiterate; but that would be expected of a man of his class at that time. He helped in disguising Charles (he was said to be similarly tall), providing him with a pair of his breeches and a doublet, and also acting as hairdresser to get rid of the king's flowing dark locks.

He was on hand for Charles in the famous oak tree episode and was his guide when the king decided to try to get to Wales. He made the long trip to London shortly after Charles returned to England to claim his crown, where he received the reception described above. His annuity was rather less than those of William and John, but unlike John he seemed to do perfectly well on it. Although continuing to live at Hobbal Grange. Richard made several return trips to London to reacquaint himself with Charles, but it led to his undoing because he caught a fever on just such a trip in February 1672, which proved fatal. He was probably in his mid-sixties.

Next came *Humphry*, the miller. He wasn't as actively involved as his elder brothers, but when he formed part of the Penderel guard escorting Charles from Boscobel to Moseley, it was his mill horse that Charles rode.

He received the same annuity (just under £70) as Richard and also rose to the status of yeoman. But he too got into financial difficulties (partly put down to having a large family) and had to petition Charles for extra funds. The king obliged and also found a post for one of his sons in the royal court (as footman to the queen consort). Like William, he lived to a good age. The year of his death varies in different accounts, but he is said to have lived to the age of at least 84.

The baby of the group was *George*. He had also served in the civil war, but by the time Charles turned up at White Ladies he was employed as a servant there. His stock rose like those of most of his brothers, and he was even appointed as one of the overseers of the poor for Cannock after the Restoration. This didn't prevent him from being hounded by the authorities for his Catholic beliefs at the time of the Popish Plot, but he eventually received the protection noted above which applied to all the Penderels. He died in approximately 1684.

Those are the Penderel brothers who took part in our story. Father Huddleston, in his reflections on this period, thought there might be a sixth brother but couldn't be sure. In fact, he was right, but could be forgiven his uncertainty. Thomas Penderel was in all likelihood abroad when Charles was fleeing the Battle of Worcester. He also fought for the Royalists during the Civil War, and was listed as killed after the Battle of Stow-on-the-Wold, six years before Worcester. However, records show that he drew up a will in Barbados in 1669, and it is now thought that he had been taken there as a prisoner to work in the sugar plantations. How much of this the other brothers or other members of his family were aware of isn't known.

Appendix B

Petitioners to the King

A selection of petitions from people claiming to have aided Charles during his escape in the Calendar of State Papers (with results where known).

Mary Graves

> ...humbly showeth that she, being the person which sent His Majesty the 12 horses, two being empty horses, the other 10 furnished with men...with a small sum of money, not worth mentioning, neither is any of this, but let His Majesty understand what hath emboldened me to presume so far; I was told that one of the horses was shot under His Majesty, and the other was that happy horse His Majesty got from Worcester upon, for which I hope my God will be pleased to make me thankful, although I have been as great a sufferer as could be, and save my life, which was often in danger of being taken from me, I having been in prison and upon bail three years after the fight at Worcester, till which time as I had taken from me and sold six hundred pounds a year, and then after they had got all I had, with much ado I got my liberty... [She then reminds Charles that she was responsible for:] sending the man, Francis Yates, to conduct your Majesty out of Worcester to White Ladies, for which doing the said Yates being hanged, your petitioner hath ever since been forced to keep his wife and five children... For doing so she hath been utterly ruined and undone, her losses and sufferings to above the value of £30,000.

There was a letter backing up her claim by no less than Richard Penderel.

Award: For a Privy Seal to confirm her grant of a forth part of such sums as are brought in by virtue of commissions for discoveries, till the sum of £30,000 is paid.

Dr Samuel Annesley, Lecturer at St Paul's, London

> Most humbly showeth that upon your Majesty's petitioner's public detesting the horrid murder of your Royal father, his refusing the engagemt. & his persuading others against it; his peremptory refusal to send out a horse against your Majesty at Worcester; his sending a man above 40 miles…to seize upon the keys of the church, to prevent one that would, against his consent, have kept the day of thanksgiving for their success at Worcester; and upon his several times saying to some of note in the army, that God would discover Cromwell to be the arrantest hypocrite that ever the Church of Christ was pestered with… Upon these & other such expressions…your Majesty's petitioner was necessitated to quit the parsonage worth between £200 & £300 per ann…

Marked: His Majesty's pleasure is, That the petitioner may be continued in the said lecture, but for salary His Majesty knows nothing of it, nor is obliged to pay it.

John Bevan of Worcester

> [Petitioning for] a Poor Knight's Place at Windsor. Was wounded in the wars, and plundered of all he had, after His Majesty's departure from Worcester; if there be no vacancy, prays that some of Cromwell's knights may be displaced.

Thomas Cock, student in physic

> For a *mandamus* to the University to grant him a Doctor's degree, being of doctor's standing. Was taken prisoner at Worcester fight, on suspicion of being the King.

Grace Moore

For the office of Searcher of Customs at Bristol for her husband. Hazarded her life and the ruin of her family, in gaining intelligence from the enemy's quarters, for His Majesty after the Battle of Worcester.

Hugh Robertson of Ireland

For some preferment. Providence has bestowed on him divers arts. One of which is how to make an engine of great use in war, which he…wished to have used at Worcester fight. Learned in Amsterdam how to make gold leather more bright than gold; is willing to impart these arts, but wants a house of art, wherein he may bring all good things to light for His Majesty's services.

Bibliography

ABBOT, Jacob, *History of King Charles the Second of England.* Harper & Bros., New York 1854 (Google Books)

ANON., *A Handbook for Travellers in Gloucestershire, Herefordshire and Worcestershire.* John Murray, London 1867 (Google Books)

ANON., *A Handbook for Travellers in Wiltshire, Dorsetshire & Somerset John*, Murray, London 1856 (Google Books)

ANON., *Memoirs of the Life of Sir Stephen Fox,* John Sackfield 1717 (Google Books)

ANON., *The Whole Series of all that hath been Transacted in the House of Peers Concerning the Popish Plot,* J Redmayne, London 1681 (Google Books)

ANON., *Transactions of the Shropshire Archaeological & Natural History Society* (Vol VII), Adnitt & Naunton, Oswestry 1907 (Internet Archive)

ATKIN, Malcolm, *Worcester 1651.* Pen & Sword, Barnsley 2008

BERESFORD, W. Rev. (ed.), *Memorials of Old Staffordshire,* George Allen & Sons, London 1909 (Internet Archive)

BISHOP, John George, *A Peep into the Past: Brighton in the Olden Time*, published by the author, 1880 (Internet Archive)

BLACKER, Rev. Beaver H., *Gloucestershire Notes & Queries* (Vol. I) W Kent & Co., London 1881 (Internet Archive)

BOYLE, The Very Revd. G.D., *Characters & Episodes of the Great Rebellion,* Clarendon Press, Oxford 1889 (Internet Archive)

BRETT, A.C.A., *Charles II & His Court,* Methuen, London 1910 (Internet Archive)

BRIGHT, Rev. Mynors (ed.), *The Diary of Samuel Pepys*, George Bell & Sons, London 1893 (Internet Archive)

BROADLEY, A.M., *The Royal Miracle,* Stanley Paul & Co., London 1912 (Internet Archive)

BUCHAN, John, *A Book of Escapes & Hurried Journeys,* Thomas Nelson & Sons 1922 (Project Gutenberg)

BURGESS, J. Tom, *Historic Warwickshire,* Simpkin, Marshall & Co., London 1876 (Internet Archive)

CARY, Henry, *Memorials of the Great Civil War in England from 1646 to 1652* (Vol II), Henry Colburn London 1842 (Internet Archive)

DALRYMPLE, D., *An Account of the Preservation of King Charles II,* 1803 (Google Books)

EVERETT GREEN, **Mary Anne** (ed.) *Calendar of State Papers, Domestic Series, of the Reign of Charles II 1660-1661,* Longman, Green, Longman & Roberts 1860 (Google Books)

FALKUS, Christopher, *The Life & Times of Charles II.* Wedenfeld & Nicholson, London 1972

FEA, Allan, *After Worcester Fight: Being a Companion Volume to "The Flight of the King",* (Internet Archive)

FEA, Allan, *The Flight of the King,* (Methuen, London 1897 (Internet Archive)

GOMME, G.L., (ed.)., *The Gentleman's Magazine Library,* Elliot Stock, London 1889 (Internet Archive)

GOUNTER, George, *The Last Act of the Miraculous Story of His Majesty King Charles the Second's Escape,* J. Russell Smith, London 1873 (Google Books)

GREENBERG, Daniel, *Comparative Regicides: King Charles I of England and King Louis XVI of France,* (Thesis) Wesleyan University, Middletown, Connecticut 2014

HARPER, Charles G, *Summer Days in Shakespeare Land,* Chapman & Hall, London 1913. (Gutenberg).

HUGHES, J. (ed.), *The Boscobel Tracts,* William Blackwood & Sons, London 1857 (Internet Archive)

JEWITT, Llewellyn Frederick William; Cox John Charles; Allen, John Romilly, *The Reliquary & Illustrated Archaeologist* (Vol XV 1874-75), Bemrose & Sons, London 1875 (Google Books)

JORDAN, Don & WALSH, Michael, *The King's Bed: Sex, Power & the Court of Charles II.* Little, Brown, London 2015

KEEBLE, N.H. (ed.), *The Autobiography of Richard Baxter,* J.M. Dent, London 1974 (Internet Archive)

LATHAM R.C., **Matthews W**. (eds), *The Diary of Samuel Pepys.* HarperCollins, London 1995

LOWER, Mark Anthony, *The Worthies of Sussex,* privately printed, 1865 (Google Books)

MASSIE, Allan, *The Royal Stuarts.* Jonathan Cape, London 2010

BIBLIOGRAPHY

MATIKKALA, Anita, *The Orders of Knighthood & the Formation of the British Honours System*. Boydell, Woodbridge 2008

MATTHEWS, William (ed.), *Charles II's Escape from Worcester,* University of California Press, Berkeley & Los Angeles 1966 (Google Books)

MONTPENSIER, Anne-Marie Louise d'Orleans, *Memoirs of Mademoiselle de Montpensier* (Vol. I) Henry Colburn, London 1848 (Google Books)

OLLARD, Richard, *The Escape of King Charles II*. Hodder & Stoughton, London, 1966

OLLARD, Richard, *The Image of the King: Charles I & Charles II*. Hodder & Stoughton, London 1979.

PORTER, Linda, *Royal Renegades: The Children of Charles I & the English Civil Wars*. Pan Macmillan, London 2017.

ROBERTS, G., *The History of Lyme Regis*, Langdon & Harker, Sherborne 1823 (Google Books)

ROBERTS, Keith, *Cromwell's War Machine: The New Model Army 1645-1660*. Pen & Sword, Barnsley, 2005.

ROOTS, Ivan, *The Great Rebellion – A Short History of the English Civil War & Interregnum 1642-60*. The History Press, Stroud 2009

SANBORN, V.C., *Genealogy of the Family of Samborne or Sanborn in England and America 1194-1898, 1899*, privately published (Wikimedia)

SCOTT, Eva, *The King in Exile,* E.P. Dutton, New York 1905 (Internet Archive)

SCOTT, William, *Stourbridge & its Vicinity,* privately published 1832 (Google Books)

SPENCER, Charles, *To Catch a King: Charles II's Great Escape*. William Collins, London 2017

STANLEY, James, *Earl of Derby: Memoirs of James, Earl of Derby,* J. Fowler, Ormskirk 1804 (Google Books)

THOMAS, Roy Digby, *Digby: The Gunpowder Plotter's Legacy*. Janus, London 2001

THOMAS-STANFORD, Charles, *Sussex in the Great Civil War & the Interregnum,* Chiswick Press, London 1910 (Internet Archive)

TOMALIN, Claire, *Samuel Pepys – The Unequalled Self*. Penguin, London 2002

WEAVER, Frederic William; MAYO, Charles Herbert, *Notes & Queries for Somerset & Dorset* (Vol. III) 1893 (Google Books)

WILLIS BUND, John, *The Civil War in Worcestershire 1642-1646; & the Scotch Invasion of 1651,* The Midland Educational Co., Birmingham, 1905 (Internet Archive)

WILLMORE, Frederic W., *A History of Walsall,* W Henry Robinson, London 1887 (Internet Archive)

Principal Websites

Battle of Worcester Society (thebattleofworcestersociety.org.uk)
British Civil War Project (http://bcw-project.org/)
British History Online (british-history.ac.uk)
Google Books (books.google.com)
Heyerlist (heyerlist.org/whos-who/Royal_Escape.html)
Internet Archive (archivc.org/indcx.php)
Oxford Dictionary of National Biography (oxforddnb.com)
Parliamentary History (historyofParliamentonline.org
Project Gutenberg (gutenberg.org)
Route Of King Charles II Through Sussex During His Flight in 1651 (pastfinders.com/sussexhistory/charles_ii.htm)